WALKING PATH: LIV...
THE JOURNEY

To Georgie

May you pathway
be full of

love.

Lucia
x

WALKING THE PATH: LIVING THE JOURNEY

LUCIA DEVANGELIO

Copyright © 2020 Lucia Devangelio
All rights reserved
FIRST EDITION

ISBN:9798689542560

Dedication

For Gino, even though our beliefs differed you still
encouraged me to finish this book.
For Jenny, you opened a door for me which I will never
close.

Acknowledgement

I wish to thank so many people that have supported me and encouraged me along the way. Ricky and Graham for their help in the early days helping to key in some information on a manual typewriter. The Circle members who without their dedication to the Circle this book would not have been possible. Michael who gave his time and proofread the manuscript. Finally, my Spirit communicators, for without them this book would not have existed at all.

Table of Contents

Introduction

These teachings were recorded and channelled by a Spirit Guide called Khan. Khan was a Mongolian Silk Trader in his previous lifetime. He lived in a city called Xi'an, in China. At that time China was ruled by the Han Dynasty from 206BC to 220AD (BCE and CE). It was a time that the Silk Road ran through the Gobi Desert which was lush and green. Khan followed the teachings of Confucius. Khan resides in the Second Spiritual Realm and the only way he can reach us to communicate with us is through another Spirit Guide named Bhatti. Bhatti is from the First Spiritual Realm. He is of a level nearer to our earthly plane.

Khan has stated that many of his teachings for us are taken from the Nazarene (Khan refers to him by this name, but we know him as Jesus).

Bhatti had a previous earthly life as a Buddhist monk and is the link between Khan and our world. Some of the words that Bhatti uses are from his Buddhist influence as a Buddhist monk. He translates the messages and channels them through the Trance Medium within our Group. Bhatti can only use terms and words that the Trance Medium has or knows as he cannot use words that the trance medium does not understand. As the next world is a world of thought.

The Spirit guides wanted these words to be put into a book form for people to read. They were also hoping for another book to be written specifically channelled for Scientists to prove the existence of Spirit. This may be a project for the future.

I have tried to keep as much of the natural conversation with Khan as possible. However, I may have had to alter some of the wording to make it easier to understand what the Spirit Guides were trying to convey, but, I hope that when putting these teachings together I have done this in a way, that is easy for most people to understand.

With some of Khan's teachings as you read them you will come across some repetitions within different Chapters. I have also included some teachings in Question-and-Answer form. The term Garden which is used a lot is an allegorical term referring to each person's lifetime and which is made up of different earthly experiences. People or souls are represented by flowers within that garden. 'Buddha' is mentioned within his teachings which represents 'the enlightened'. 'Bodhisattva' is on the pathway to enlightenment.

"If these words fit within your life and enrich your life, drink of it as you will, so it may nourish the seed within, so that your own spiritual growth will come into bloom. But take only from these words that which you need and question all. Do not accept anything until you have questioned. This is not the ONLY truth but one of many truths. If you find these words do not fit in with your life, then it is not for you… I hope and pray that you will find your pathway. But remember Question All. Only then, will you find what is right for you."
khan

Foreword from Khan

I do not teach the powers of discernment, the powers of prophesy. My job is to teach you how to use the power within you, which is available to all, by giving you some insight into the laws, the natural laws, which all must live by in life. You cannot know how to use the powers if you do not know where to look, so it falls upon me to try to show to you the different and varied paths, which lead to the same source. For, you may be able to gain some brief enlightenment once on the nature of your own path, for each of you tread different paths, but you must need light to show you the way, for you cannot find things in a darkened room. You need illumination to find things; through illumination you will see the power that abounds all around you. Within each of you is the power of the universe which some call God, which some call 'The Spirit'. Each of you are from that same source, but because of your physical lives you lose contact with the source, you find it impossible to see things of a spiritual nature. Only by teachings and illuminations will you know in which place to look for this source-once you have gained the state of Buddha (the enlightened).

Each of you must look within your heart for this creative power, for the power which abounds all around you in everything. It is the natural law of the universe. For within each of you is your own spiritual body. Many times, your own spiritual body prompts and tells you which is the right way. For you feel which is good within your world. You feel your way through life, if your heart is open. Only in this way will you gain the insight into the natural laws, into the Prana, and words in which to use this. You must refine yourselves. You must question everything which you will hear, you must question everything which people tell you. You will come across many teachers, many Masters in your life on the physical world. You must question everything, for many say they have the right answers; but only if the answers enrich your life, only if you can see good in the answer which you have asked, then you will use this, for it is good. If it fits within your world and if it fits within your life, then it is a teaching of the good side of the power. Many get confused within your world, they only see one aspect of the whole and they say this is the right way which you should all tread. It is wrong to be forced down one road. You must find your own pathways within your life, you must live your own lives not the experiences of others, for they are experiences outside your own knowledge. Each of you have your own pathways. You must not judge others.

There are many souls trying to carry out the work within your world, but there are many of an unenlightened nature. This is their own path, they try to the best of their abilities, but there are many within your world who try to falsify what they know, they try to mislead people, they try to benefit from the unenlightened souls within your world.

It is not wrong to question, for whether you believe or not, in the things which I say, I only ask you to try the things in your life if they are a benefit to you; then, obviously these things must be good. But if you find these things in which I speak are not of benefit to you, then, they are wrong for you.

People say that they are afraid to give out love because they get hurt. But surely then the love which they give out is of a selfish nature. It is not the true love of spirit. For you do not love to be loved. You love to be. You must not ask for things in return for what you give. I am also asked why, when love and trust is given but then this trust is abused, again they are hurt. Your heart should be enlightened. Their hearts may not be enlightened. You must not feel hurt or guilty. If they do not accept the understanding and loyalty which you have, if they wish to turn their back on the light, then this is their choice, for it is these souls which will find themselves in the Winterlands. They are still looking at things from a physical nature, but you do not have to be of the physical world.

Within each of you lies the true nature of spirit, within each of you is the pure bounteous light of all creation, within each of you are all the answers of everything which you care to ask. The only thing which stops you from gaining these answers and gaining this light is the physical world, the misconceptions and the false teachings of the physical world. It is all about you, you must look at nature, you must look at the animal kingdom and learn to be.

When a soul is born into your world, we class this as a passing, as they leave us. When a soul leaves your world, we class this as a birth within our world, for it is only an example, it is a testing time. You have been brought up with creeds and stigmas through false teachers, who we have mentioned before. We grow impatient of these teachers; we grow impatient of these types of lies which are forced upon others. It is wrong to force your opinions; it is wrong to force your way of life on any other soul within your world. You can voice an opinion; you can discuss an opinion, but it is wrong to force an opinion. It is wrong to force your children to think the same as yourself. It is wrong to force them to do what you want them to do. Once this lesson has been learnt, life within the physical world would be heaven. Through people of a like-mind, who are willing to hold the lantern for knowledge, this will come about.

There have been many misconceptions. The early lantern bearers in this world also had their misconceptions, for they tried to force the Jesus figure on everybody. He is only one of many teachers, who must be regarded in the same light as The Buddha, The Prophet Mohammad, Krishna and many others. They are all of a like mind, they are all friends, they taught the same, they taught in a simple way, so people could understand simplicity. They did not try to make things confusing to people, for if they did, nobody would understand what they were trying to do.

It is only the physical world which makes things complicated, which hides behind blinds of closed doors. The doors must be burst open. They are old dogmas and the old superstitions. There is a new feeling within your world, do not let it pass. There is a new realisation within your world. The suffering within your world will cease, so there will be no need for people, no need for souls to enter your world. For souls will be able to progress to go to higher things, instead of being held back by the same old desires and cravings which they learnt within your world.

Also understand, that there are many souls who do return to your world who reside in the Summerland's. There are also many souls who return to your world who reside in the First Kingdom. These souls are of a lesser evolved nature, they feel that their feelings are still close to the earth. They have not yet learnt to pass that stage. So, they return to learn more lessons to help them progress to the Summerland's and higher. In the Summerland's you learn to drop all your physical attributes and learn about the spirit world. There are also souls who are of a less evolved nature and who reside in the Winterlands, this is where a great deal of our spirit work is carried out.

There will be a new awakening. There are many souls within your world who are lost, the pace of your life seems to be too fast for them. They are seeking alternatives. Many are going back to the natural way of living. Many are going back to older beliefs, they are seeking out the old gods, many are turning to religion. There is a new feel about your world, that at along last you are seeing and realising the horrors of your world and thinking that there is a way to stop this by a change of attitude. Not by forceful ways, not by crushing the evil forces. You cannot do it this way, by crushing evil. You must need force to crush evil, therefore you are causing the same conditions within yourself that you are trying to cease. You give love and compassion and understanding, but it will take longer this way.

We tried to bring about the movement many years ago, which fell on stony ground. For people did not understand. The youth used to sing and shout about love, but now there is a new feeling within your world. Many people are realising: these people want to know. They want to find out for themselves. They are the Lantern Bearers. You can look around, there is a new movement within your political world, there is a movement within the young of your world, music plays a great part in this. So, therefore it is important that all forms of communication are there for the asking. The law of Karma also affects material things.

You can only live one day at a time for there is only one day for you to live at a time. You do not live five or six days every day. You must look around your world and pick your lessons. They are there. There are many lessons you overlook. You must also think that the lives that you lead are of your own making. You choose the time and the place and the life which you live I will say many times it is of your own making.

Life is not what you see through your eyes. Life is what you feel. For the biggest problem within your world is to teach people that they are not what they see in the mirror. The people they see are two-dimensional people, they do not see their inner self, they cannot think of things to come and things past. They were spirit and they are spirit and they will always be spirit. There is no death as you call it.

1: Karma

Q*uestioner*: "Would it be spiritually beneficial to understand previous lives and previous incarnations, so we could sort out our karma in this life, the reason why we're here? Would this make our spiritual progression easier?"

Khan: "Every child who is born has perfect knowledge of the Spirit World and the previous incarnations. We use the knowledge of the mind, we can only use what is only in the mind, that is why it is hard. We learn. We are grateful. Each child has a perfect knowledge, but through the teachings of your physical world, they are scorned, they are told not to seek that life, they are told to stop making up and to stop to lie.

So you have the knowledge within each of you and by seeking this knowledge, you are seeking this spiritual knowledge, for in your past lives you will find your past struggles, and by seeking your past struggles you can see the faults within each of you and by seeing the faults within each of you, you can judge what is right and what is wrong and you can also see that light of Spirit and you can see for yourselves the truth in these words. You have spiritual bodies which relate to the seventh kingdom. So therefore, you must have seven individual bodies, which you will use at various times in your progression through lives. I will try to give you some other geography of these bodies within each of you. You know of only two of these bodies, you only know of the physical and the purely spiritual body. The spiritual body is the one that prompts and gives you inner guidance. 'Your own inner voice'. Your own inner voice is your actual spiritual body trying to direct and guide. That is why it is important to listen to your instincts and your own inner voice. But these bodies are not within each of you, this may seem hard to understand, but there are seven different levels and each of your seven bodies reside on a different spiritual plane. There is only one consciousness and at the present this consciousness resides within the physical body, when the physical body's lifespan is fulfilled, the consciousness will drift into the next body.

Within your world, you see all around you the physical world, but overlaid is each of the Spiritual Worlds, they are in your world, but they are not in your world. If you can grasp this idea then you can grasp the idea of separate bodies residing on each of the planes, but because your consciousness is all in one body, then you must search your next body. It mimics the actions which you show in this world, that is why it is important to bring about in your world a spiritual realisation, for any wrong actions within your world, will bring about the law of karma.

The law of Karma comes from the other spiritual realms. Any action within this world will cause

effects in the next worlds. But because your consciousness is within your own physical world you cannot see the repercussions of your actions within the spiritual world. There is only one means for you to know the happening of each of the spiritual worlds and that is through listening to your own inner self which resides on the highest realm, because this body is pure light and pure understanding can filter through to the physical world in some form.

Through the opening of your consciousness and accepting this fact, you can let more light through into your world from your own higher self. These may seem hard facts, you may not agree with these facts, but they are as I see them. You must understand that every word spoken, every act has its' own effects. When a word is spoken that word takes reality. Once that word is spoken there is no calling that word back. That word will move outwards until it resides in some other consciousness, and you will feel the repercussions of any wrong word or action caused in your world. That is why we (spirit) teach, that is why it is not important to stand within your churches, telling people what they will and will not see, but it is important to give out the philosophies of life, to give out the guidelines.

You all need something to hold on to within this life, make sure that the things that you hold dear are true and the things that you have lost are for the benefit of others, for benefitting others you benefit yourselves in the long run. For the law of Karma, you will receive all you give out. Be the judge only of yourselves, always question, always seek from life the answers and the lessons, for nothing happens within your world without a specific purpose, and through the light of knowledge, you will judge all things fairly within yourselves. You must seek out your higher selves, you must seek out the true spiritual self which resides within all. This is the spark of life. From whilst you came you will return but depending on the lessons you
learnt depends on the length of time it takes to return"

2: Children and the Spirit World

All children see the Spirit World, as they grow older, they are subjected to the doctrines and teachings of teachers of the Physical World, that they lose their sense of perception.

Children have a very great understanding of things. They are much more in tune with our side than the adults of your world. All children are very spiritual people, they have great insight into things. The adult world can learn a great deal by listening to the children of your world. Children accept all things. Make sure that they accept the right things.

You would not feed them grass, you feed them the correct things. It is the same with the mind, do not feed them rubbish. Always seek the highest. Do not worry about the children, they will find their own paths, for they chose their own parents.

3: Problems

Try to remember that you have chosen this life, that before you entered the physical world you chose this time. You are living in the physical world, but there is another image of your life within the spiritual world. It is like an echo of the life which you make now. This echo will go from birth to death. We can see the pathway of your life for you choose this yourself. It is like a blueprint of your life which resides on our side of things.

All you have to do is to contact your higher self and you would be in control of your life and you would know each step which you are going to take and which you wish to take, that which you planned before you entered into this life. There is also the way in which you could enrich yourself with the material trappings. You must decide on how to use this. Whether it is for self-need or self-greed. If your heart is pure and your mind is clear, then all will go well. For we do not expect you to live a purely spiritual life within your world, you have to lead the physical life as well, because you must understand that the more of the physical trappings which you gather around you the more of the physical problems you will have in the physical world for we see this from our side.

All you must do is to remember this. If you lead a simple life you will have simple problems, if you do not wish to lead a simple life then you should expect the hard and the trying problems. Do not complain to us. We will stand by you, but you should never blame us for your own situation. If you made the wrong decisions, we would still be with you. We will never leave you alone for we cannot. You must never be too serious; you must always look to the brighter side of things. You, in your problems, are much helped through laughing, for through laughter is your own release mechanism within you which will lift you above the problems and lighten your spirits. Never worry about the problems which you have, for you will always have problems of a degree or another, so why worry about them!

When you learn to cease to worry about your problems you will find you have no problems and you do not worry about them, so you will not have any problems.

We will never leave you alone, for we are part of you, and you are part of us. If you pass metal through the fire it hardens the metal and it will not break. This is what all your problems do to you if you would only realise this. If you have worries over the material side, these are not worries, these are nothing, for you leave these things behind you. The only worries you should have is whether you are doing what is spiritually right.

These are the only worries that you should have, that these are the only problems that you should be fearful over. But it is hard to see when you are blindfold, and we appreciate your problems. We just try to make you realise, that is all, for we still love you. You would not, in your garden, pull out a beautiful flower because it is in the wrong place, would you? You would still cherish it, no matter what side of the fence it was on. You are all beautiful flowers to us. Our only concern is to see you grow. Your scents may vary, your colours may vary but you all have that universal spirit. We do not want everybody to be the same, to act the same. It would be too easy; it would be boring. You all have your own life, you all have your own individuality, you all have your own different things to contribute to others. We all feed off each other, we all give, this is why there are many different voices within the choir, but it is still a beautiful noise. You must attune yourself into life, you must attune yourself into the natural flow of things. Do not fight against what you feel is natural and all will be well in the end, all will be harmonious.

All life is music, and music is life, for without the music - without vibration you are nothing. There is no life without music, is there not? There is no music without life. By touching the right notes and the right chords you can become in balance with other souls. Use the music of life to clear away the debris of your daily living and the daily debris of your souls.

'God Bless you all, I would like to say, as the love flows through, we wish to talk of tolerance amongst you, and amongst all the people of your earth plane, we ask only that you keep your hearts open to the other vibrations on your earth plane, that you may give out only your love and never judge, and never condemn another fellow man.

The true work is love, there are many people in their development at different levels and it is hard for you to understand their plight, but you must be patient with these people, my friends, they need your understanding and your love, there is much hurt and many cruel words spoken.

You understand, just remember, never to judge others" … Khan

4: Living your Life upon the Physical World

If somebody within your world strikes you upon the face, thank them. If somebody within your world takes a possession of yours, thank them. If you have arranged a meeting with somebody and they do not show, thank them. For these are all lessons. Do not judge, do not look for what is not there. You must live your life for each moment, you must not look at what could have been or what may be.

You live complicated lives within the physical world. Your complicated lives are made by you. Life is simple, all you must do is accept and live. Living comes easy. You cannot help but live, but you make life complicated, you will never cease to live, so you must accept life as natural and just go with the life which you have. You must listen with the heart, you must feel with the heart, you must see with the heart. Do not feel with the physical body. Do not see with the physical body. You can't see the Spirit World with physical eyes, you must see with the heart. Your lives are complicated, but you must realise you make them so. When you can live a life which is not complicated, then you will cease to need more lives within the physical world, once you will accept that simple lives bring simple problems, complicated lives bring complicated problems.

In your world you are living in the physical world, you are living with the physical mind and the spiritual heart. We speak about the flowers in the garden using them as an example, to explain life, watch the flowers, for the flowers grow by themselves. They are simple things, they just grow, and they are beautiful. If you would allow yourselves to just simply grow, each of you would be beautiful.

You complicate your lives, you make your own worries, you blame others, you blame spirit, you blame countless things, you also blame yourselves. This blocks the heart.

Simplicity in all things, all teachings are simple, all knowledge is simple, if you will allow it to be so. There are many things in your world which block us, which block the teachings and put obstacles in your life.

Nishkam Karma (conscientious action) is the path of selflessness, to be able to be the true bodhisattva (a person who has attained Enlightenment, but who postpones Nirvana in order to help others to attain Enlightenment). You must use the energy which you put into Nishkam Karma. You must all accept and use the energy, for each of you puts much energy into wrongful things. To be the true Buddha (enlightened one) you must put behind you all the chains and shackles of your life. The hardest thing in your life is the Nishkam Karma, the path of selflessness. For you want things in your world. It is not wrong to want things but be on your guard that you do not make these into obsessions. For through obsessions you become single-minded and disregard everything else. The energy which you put into these obsessions can be used to your benefit, if you realise at the time of your obsessions and build your own life. You make your own mountains which you will climb. You waste much prana. (energy, life-force).

The true aim in your life must be to gain the freedom of the mind, so you are able to think, so you are able to use your natural powers, and the result will be for the good of others, so you can spread the Buddha life. You cannot find your heart's desire in the dark. You must help the light, for within the light there is recognition of all things which you need and which you desire for a good and righteous life. You must be single minded. Your mind must be sharp, it must be single pointed. As the arrow travels swift and sharp to its' target, so should your mind. You must not complain at your short comings, you must not blame others for the life which you lead, for ultimately you must recognise Nishkam Karma within your lives. And use the energies. You must follow the dharma, for it shows all things.

You must look at all things, when you look at your world. Your world is a balanced world for it goes through four seasons. Your lives also go through seasons. When you are in the Summertime everything looks nice, everything has the appearance of well-being. Then you go through the mournful time of Autumn a reflective time when you think of things that have passed in the Summertime. Then you go to the deep heart of Winter – the sleeping period, where everything looks at its worst. Then you have the promise of Spring and you can see the Summertime approaching once more. Your lives rotate in the same manner.

When you have no problems, you are in your own Summertime, but do not forget that following Summertime there is Autumn and Winter. All things follow this cycle. Be prepared next time you are feeling low, unhappy or you have sunk first to the depths of despair. When you are in the depths of despair, always remember that Summertime always follows Winter. Day always follows Night. These are from the mental principles and concepts. These are the rules of spirit and of your world. These are the basis of all life. Try and remember this in your problems and may they give you help and encouragement. Even the most beautiful of flowers must go through the wintertime. A time of death. But it is soon reborn again in the Spring and then Summertime.

Who are you? You are not who you think you are! You are Spirit! Some people in your lives, may not know or be aware of the celestial light. That does not mean, because you do that your soul is any more developed than theirs. You must look at their aura, you must look at what they give. Do not give to receive, this is wrong. You must love unselfishly. You must be of the world but not in the world, (as so many of your teachers have said), You must work, you must help others and ask nothing in return. By giving, your soul will grow. By giving, your soul will develop. By giving your love will increase. By giving you will bring together your Soul Group. We have no use for the man who has great spiritual knowledge, who sits and meditates, who thinks only of himself. The man who looks at the starving and thinks how developed he is, has nothing for those souls.

We would like to see people give their lives to others; you must develop yourselves so you can help others. People may find their own paths of enlightenment and must find their own way. I plant the seed. You must cultivate your own garden before you can criticise your neighbours.

5: Chakras, Colours and Healing

Colour plays in important part in your everyday life. Colour is one of the predominant things in your life, you must learn to see and to feel and to use the colour. We refer to the seven centres within your bodies. These are the ones that diffuse the light of the Spirit World to a different part of your body to be used by the different centres. The main centres. There are seven colours, there are seven main centres. Within your rainbow you see the seven colours you can experience these colours within your healing, within your work. These colours are the most important part of your work. By experiencing these colours, by using these colours, you advance yourself and you will be ready for the work within your First Heaven, where colour and thought predominate.

If you take the physical colour of you all Yellow and you take the colour Blue and you mix the two colours, like all painters do, you get the earth colour Green, which is a peace colour. You must learn to use colour in your work, you must awake your spirit of the child within you, and of the animal world. For you can learn many things by looking at nature through the eyes of your inner child, for you have forgotten the innocence within you all.

Each one of your senses works off a different colour. Your main centre is what you call the Solar Plexus. The word

Solar comes from the body that lies amid your planetary system. It is the body which gives off light. It gives off the White light which is made up of all colours.

In your meditations many of you see a White light, many of you see yourselves stood in the light. You receive this light in your Solar Plexus which divides the colours to your other senses starting with your Base centre (Genital Area), which is Red, a very strong colour, a very needful colour, but a colour that must not be used by itself. It is related to the base of your being and relates to the base of your emotions. An earthly colour.

The next of your senses lies within your Stomach which is the Orange. People who use meditation within their lives, and are conscious of their bodies through their diets, rely on this centre and this colour. This centre relates to your Stomach which changes the foods of your world into the salts and minerals which enables your body to keep the correct balance. Too much of this colour relates to your diet. Do not take this colour in excess, you must not overindulge in your diets. People who use meditation as part of their lives will often find themselves wearing this colour in their earthly garments.

The next centre is the most important centre. It is your Solar Plexus, which is Yellow in colour. This colour reflects the Spirit colour, reflects the life-giving colour from your sun which enables everything physical to grow, and reflects the spiritual colour which enables everything spiritual to grow. This is the most important of your centres.

The next centre in your bodies is your Heart Centre, whose colour is Green. This is also an important centre, and relates to your higher emotional self, which also relates to the nature and the colour of your surroundings. You must feel one with nature, you must relate the colour of the plants to the colour of your heart, you must feel at one with nature, you must feel at one with the world. This is one of the hardest colours to find within yourselves. The next colour of your body is your Throat Centre which is predominantly

Blue. This is the communication centre. In your healing you must use the colour Blue and use Spirit in that communication. Also use this colour when you explain or teach about our teachings. And when you give the divine truths you must use this colour. The next two centres in your bodies are your Mind and that centre which lies above your head which are Indigo and Violet, which are deep spiritual colours. The Violet of the Mind and the Indigo must be used in equal amounts. You must teach yourselves not only to see the colours in others and the colours within yourselves, but also to feel the colours. You must feel them, you must experience them.

These are things which Spirit can manifest in your world. Colour plays an important part in your world, and an even more important part within our world. When you see a colour, you must see within that colour all the shades and hues. When you heal you must see within that person the different shades and hues of that person, wherein you will be able to see the correct way to heal, for a lack of any colour means a lack within that centre. Dietary problems mean a lack of the Orange. Worries and anxieties can be related to the Red colour because most worries and anxieties are caused through lustful living and jealousies. Mental problems can be related to the Violets, you must study the person, you must feel the colour.

Each person receives the white light. The different centres reflect their own light in the Aura, so you will be able to see the lack or the excess of any of the centres or colours. There must be a perfect balance. Each centre must function. You cannot have any one Centre overlapping into another Centre. This will cause big problems in your physical self.

There are many more than the seven colours, but the denser atmosphere of your physical world makes it impossible for you to see these colours. When you receive these colours within your bodies through your Solar Plexus, the last of your bodies receives this as pure White light. The more you develop the more you can take within you the colours of the Spirit World. The more your spirit body which lies deep within you will radiate. The more these colours in your aura join, the more your aura will show the Golden light. Everything is symbolic and everything can be seen with your development. We ask you to search in this area for wisdom for in this area lies a bounteous place of knowledge and wisdom.

6: Working with colour

Q*uestioner*: "When I meditate or sit in a group situation working with spirit, when we have a red light on, I seem to have more awareness with the red light, I see transfigurations … why is that?"

Khan: "It is a physical colour, it is the colour of your base chakra, so the effects from this would be of the physical nature, if you are trying to work with spirit, or any form of spiritual practice within the red light, then you will get physical reactions. You could work with green light it would be more on the emotional level or it would refer to your heart. So, you would feel, more, than you would see. If you work with the purple light, you will get more philosophy within your mind. If you work with the blue light, you will attract the healing power to you. You have seven beings, your outer being which you refer to as yourself, your physical self relates to the Red chakra. It is the most physical centre within yourself. So, it is the first of your bodies, you must try to think of it as a journey home. This is the first stage.

The second stage, you have an inner body which is orange, which is one step removed from your physical world, but which is still connected to the physical world, for it needs nourishment, it is still connected with the Red. It is one step removed from the red, but it still needs to be fed.

The next one is a body of energy, you need energy within the physical world, not just physical energy but you need energy from all around. This is the Solar Plexus, but it also a body of energy within you. It like taking off overcoats.

The next centre is the heart centre, but also a physical or should I say a body within you. Your emotional body. connected to all your centres. As you pass from your physical world, the body which you shed is the red body, and you are left with six centres, as you pass into your second kingdom, you shed your orange body, so you survive on the energy, the emotion, the healing, your consciousness and your spiritual self. This is where it begins to get hard, for you must learn through reincarnation after reincarnation how to escape from the physical and your first kingdom. When you break this cycle, you pass into your third kingdom and you lose one more of yourself, and you live on the emotional level, not the power nature, you live an emotional nature, with healing, intelligence and spirituality. And as you lose each one after each one until you regain that spiritual being which resides on the highest plane, which is your higher self, which if also your pure purple being. This is your link with what you might call the highest heaven. So, by using the colours within your physical world you can attain any level of kingdom you wish, if you have the tools and the understanding."

Questioner: "When you say getting in touch with our higher self, what do you mean by the higher self? Your actual Inner Spirit when you get to the purple?"

Khan: "The purple resides within you, if you imagine a purple diamond, with six colours enclosing it, as you die each one is stripped away. This is how you must think of your own body, your own self, you do not change into something, you are all seven, and we strip away the outer until we regain that of us which is pure spirit, which resides within us which people call the soul or whatever you wish to call it, it is your essence, your spiritual essence. The learning which we all undertake enables us to experience certain things which we can strip away at ourselves, at our own pace, until we are left with our pure self. The day we go into the new phase of existence, where we try to go beyond, but this I do not know.

It is only what others say, or what we all think or talk about, for we have to attain this ourselves before we can say."

Questioner: "Are you from a higher Spiritual Kingdom?"

Khan: "I have shed only two bodies. I reside within the Second Spiritual Kingdom".

Questioner: "While I am healing, I always see the colour Green. I always see these colours and not any others. Why is this?"

Khan: "Within your healing you see the green, you use your heart with your healing you draw from nature, you gain strength from the plant world and you use the violet or your mind, you use the knowledge which you have gained, you use your knowledge to determine the state of development of the person who needs the healing you draw from nature for the strength for the healing, but around you, you also draw the blue, when you do your healing for you communicate the violet knowledge and the love of your nature to the person you heal, although you might not see the blue, it radiates in your aura and we are overjoyed when you use this healing knowledge, for you draw from nature."

Questioner: "I would like to know when I see colours such as gold, violet and blue what does this mean?"

Khan: "The gold you see is the love which certain souls in spirit show for you, it is a colour which only the developed souls of the Spirit World can show to the souls of the physical world. You have loved ones in the spiritual world, when they are close to you, you may not see them as they once were, but you see them as they are now. You see the gold of the spirits. The violet is your understanding and of the work you do. The blue is the communication that you give of your knowledge."

7: Meditation

The main thing within meditation is the destruction of the ego. When you live your lives without any thought of self-gain, without any base emotions of hatred or jealousies, you will become a Buddha (the Enlightened). You will transcend all earthly things. Your consciousness will only dwell on the spiritual planes. Your body may reside in the physical world, but your heart, mind and soul will reside on the astral world. The wealth of teachings which you may gain for yourself without instruction from teachers will be yours. It is there for you to grasp, if you dare grasp this light.

There is light enough for every one of you within your world. It is hard for you to see this light, you are one small candle within a very dark world, but the more candles that are drawn together, the brighter the illuminations so all may see. There are teachings all around you of many creeds, many cultures for you to read, for you to delve into. There is a wealth of teachings and knowledge. There are many scientists coming to the same conclusions that the mystics and holy men came to teach mankind about spirituality. The more you find out, the more there is to know, and the wealth of knowledge will come together both on the scientific plane and on the spiritual plane.

Questioner: "Can we attain more knowledge through meditation?"

Khan: "You can seek your knowledge through meditation. But if your heart is strong enough and open enough you can seek this knowledge through others. You can also seek this knowledge by studying yourselves. For the faults you have are faults which you have chosen to work on, but you did not have in previous lives. Through your meditations, and through gaining stillness, you can bring to remembrance your previous lives with your previous teachings. There are many forms of meditation from all different cultures. Search for the one that gives you peace and comfort and the more you meditate the more you will feel your inner being and us around you. The bounteous love that surrounds you all. We are just a thought away."

Questioner: "When you say getting in touch with our higher self, how do we do that, is that through meditation?"

Khan: "By forgetting who you are, or who you think you are. For you are not what you think you are. Meditation will give you comfort. Where you find it hard at times, for there is a battle within you between your Base Chakra and your Highest Chakra. Your Highest Chakra is your Spiritual Self and your Base Chakra is your Physical Self and it is a tug towards one and it is a tug towards the other. If you could be aware of all your Inner selves, then you would not need to regain the earth. For you would understand the necessity of leaving behind you what you do not need. You must transcend what you think is the self and go beyond to find the essence of your being, of your nature, if you understand. It is hard, this is why you have the symbol within your sky to remind you of yourselves, the rainbow. You need to have symbols of these which you can relate to. It is given to you to remind you of who you are and not who you think you are. Therefore, these colours appear above you, so you have to look up to them, to aspire to an ideal which is above you."

8: Meditation task

Imagine you are sitting in a garden, it must be your garden that you make in your mind, and it must be the same garden all the time. You see gardens with flowers and colours. These gardens and these flowers are individual to you, because you are individuals and have individual likes and dislikes, and it is wrong for you to judge your neighbour's garden until your own garden is in order. But because you have different likes does not mean to say that your garden is not as good as your neighbour's or your neighbour's garden is not as good as your own. The plants are the same. It is the attitude which differs. You may wander around your garden, but you must get to know your garden. Do this regularly, within your thoughts, so everything has a place, so whenever you enter your garden it will always be the same, it will always be familiar to you, so you can find great peace and comfort there.

Whilst you are in this garden, this is the right time to bring your problems forward in your mind, to look at your problems. For you are comfortable and you have the power within you there, then. You will find it easy to work your problems out. So, do you think you could do this? You will find the benefits. Have the same colours and views which you like. It does not matter what sort of garden you choose, but it must be one which is favourable to you and must always look the same. It must always smell the same, and, most important, the sounds must always be the same. Whether you have music there or whether you have the natural sounds of music or the creatures which are there, it is up to you. It can be where you like, and what style you like. But there must be different sections of this garden used for specific things. If you imagine two flowers that are a darker blue, sit amongst them and try your problems, for it is the colour of the mind, you understand. If you wish just to think energy so can recharge your batteries, sit among the yellow flowers of your garden.

If you find pleasure and you feel strengthened by the Summer, feel yourself with all nature, and keep it with you at other times when nature seems to die, to enable you to live through the Winter, to the next Spring and the next hope. Use your own garden as a perpetual Summer, so you will gain strength from this as you live through the Winter of your lives and you can use the strength from your garden to strengthen you against your physical Winter life. Use the scents of the flowers and the power there from your garden. Use the imaginary garden within your mind and feel as one.

9: Soul Groups

Before your spirit body meets with its Soul Group, your spirit body is in a primitive form of evolution, you have heard of the phrase "New Souls". These souls do not just appear, these souls have experienced previous forms of existence, it is no accident that you take care of the animals, that you love the animals. The more developed you become the more sensitive you are. The reason for this is your spiritual body has inhabited the animal form, then you developed from the animal form to become a new soul.

If you feel a bond with someone and you see within that soul a likeness with yourself, and you feel at peace with that person, then this person is of a Soul Group. For the people of the Souls which are not in your Soul Group, you have trials with. You find it hard to talk, you find it hard to communicate or live with them, and in your past lives (which each of you have had many), you have been of different cultures. You have to have a varied background so you can draw on these teachings which lie dormant within each one of you but at times surface. They are prompted at the times needed. When you have passed, you judge yourself and you pass again and re-join your Soul Group. You then assess what you have learnt collectively. If you feel you have not learnt enough to go to the next Kingdom, then you will reincarnate, but it does not have to be in this form.

You cannot progress until all your Soul Group reach the stage of progression. You cannot progress until you reach the

Astral World. I believe, you can progress singularly into your First Realm and meet up with the rest of your Soul Group in the Second Realm. You then judge collectively within the Soul Group the knowledge attained in your current life experiences and what you have learnt collectively. Your Soul Group then determine whether another life is necessary or whether you want to try the next Realm or whether you want to stay in the current Realm and help others or whether you want to try new existences of a different form.

There are other worlds, there are many souls of those with life, all striving for the same as you. There are many worlds of a highly developed nature, of a more highly spiritual nature within your own role, within your own experiences. The Earth is only one of many. If you try as a Soul Group to attain the next Kingdom you will know how far your development has come. If you are not able to go forward into the next Kingdom, then you will all step back into the previous Kingdom and you must then try a new existence.

So, in your First Realm you will judge yourselves. In the Second Realm you judge the collective knowledge of your Soul Group, so it is important to gain and remember to forefront the teachings of your past lives, so you may use them in this life, or any other lives which you may choose to live, so then you may gain and store this knowledge, so when you meet with your Soul Group, you may lay bare the knowledge you have and you may find how far down the path of life you have gained.

 Each of you in your singular lives, in your physical lives, must pause and use your meditations as a form of looking back, as a form of looking at the path you have travelled, to see how far you have come. By looking back, you can see how far there is to go. There is no harm in looking back, there is no harm in remembering.

You make mistakes in your life; you do not forget these mistakes. Many say it is pointless looking at the past for the past holds no future, but we say the past is the future, the past holds the key to the future. By forgetting your mistakes, you will make them again. By remembering your mistakes, you may use these, and you will never make the mistakes again, or we hope you will never make the mistakes again!

Some of you will remember. Some will make the same mistakes repeatedly; it is in your nature. It is only up to your understanding. Your understanding must improve.

10: Soul Group Members and Reincarnation

If you feel that there is a bond between people, a bond of pure love and understanding, where there does not reside any hatred then this is the bond of a Soul Group.

You know yourselves who are members of your own Soul Group for you feel a bond with each other and the light of understanding between you. You love each other in a pure way. Individuals know who members of their Soul Group are for they feel the attraction between them, and they come together to share their problems. They will come together to help, they come together for enjoyment. For a variety of different reasons because they find great comfort in each other's presence. Each one of you are members of a Soul Group. Each time you manifest in a different experience you will feel a bond with other members of your Soul Group. Each of you go through these experiences together. In these past lives you will meet many people, but you stay closest to the people of your Soul Group because you carry these memories and these experiences over with you into other lives.

You will attract Guides and Helpers of these experiences. You attract many people of that same experience, for they feel an affinity with you because they also have experienced the same things which you have experienced.

In your physical life if you did something which enriches the heart, if you go somewhere and have a good time, this memory will stay with you longer than the bad times. So previous existences act in the same way. The physical mind tends to block out anything which is unpleasant. Not all your previous incarnations have been good, you must experience the bad as well as the good.

You are with your Soul Group many lifetimes. Sometimes you do not meet in one lifetime but are living elsewhere on a different part of your world. Most of your lives you spend together but there are some odd times that some of you are not there. Depending on the needs of the soul depends on what life you wish to have, you sometimes need different lessons. You stay with your Soul Group and you may meet many other souls of different Soul Groups. Sometimes your husband is your child in one lifetime, or your sister is your brother in the next. Everyone has a part to play each lifetime. It is dependent on what the lessons you need to learn at that lifetime.

Questioner: "What about if you are due to be born but are rejected because something is wrong?

Khan: "While you are waiting to enter the earth, or whatever reason it may be for, you are a new soul or you are regaining a new experience, you choose your parents, and you wish to take on a certain character for the tests which you have devised, it is not your fault if you are rejected. But you still have these lessons to learn, and it is important that the same parents are chosen otherwise you would have to learn other lessons.

If you desire to learn other lessons besides a specific one or you feel it is important to learn this at your stage of development, then you have to wait until it is time to come again. You will always find that there will be another birth after you are taken away. It is not specific of the soul generally, but of the new soul who wishes to depart. So, if you are not able to arrive at that place where the exam is, then you must try again next time that the exam is available to you."

11: Passing Over or Going Home

When a soul is born into your world, we class this as a passing. When a soul leaves your world, we class this as a birth.

When your time for the crossing is upon you, you will recognise this. You may feel pain, but it is only the physical pain, because the time draws near. It is like waking from a dream, you find that the pain will slowly go. You will begin to see various things from our side. They will be super-imposed over the physical world; you will find it hard to distinguish between the physical and the spiritual.

You will see many friends, you will see many relations, you will see many helpers and guides, they are there to help you, so do not be afraid when this time is upon you. It is a very gentle time. You will feel a great peace fill you, for it is your own inner bodies welcoming the time. The time of your trials are over, it is a time of a great sense of relief. Therefore, it is important that you do not grieve for those that have passed, for you fill these souls with sorrow. For the unenlightened soul feels that they should still be with you, that they should not be the cause of this grief. So, you should be happy at the time of a soul's crossing, for it is they who are benefitting.

You will feel the sinking sensation, or it may be a floating sensation, as you drift from that body. You will feel a slight pull, it is not painful, and it will not harm you, it is gentle, and it is natural, and you will recognise it as being natural. You will hear music and you will smell very sweet smells, you may see many rich colours which you never dreamt of before and you will see a brightness, a very bright light, and you will head for that light, for you know it is instinct that this is home.

As you drift towards this light, the music will continue and increase. It is a beautiful time; you are free from the restraints of the physical world. Your heart will be filled with love of a much finer degree that you could ever imagine. You will feel love with everything, for you are everything and everything is a part of you. You will feel a warmth of emotion within you for it is a home coming, and you will remember past lives, your memory will slowly return. You will remember all your trials. You will remember all your past acquaintances and you will be filled with such joy as you return to your own individual garden, which you have built within the spiritual world over many lifetimes. For every time you return to your garden, you return with fresh flowers for your garden, with fresh ideas for your garden. As your garden grows so your heart will swell, and your understanding of things will grow. It is a time of great celebration.

It is also a time of sorrow for the things which you did not learn, the past mistakes which you made, which you realise nobody will judge, only yourself. You are your own task master, and you will be hard on yourself, that is why you chose the trials which you did within the physical world.

There are many worlds, that all go through this. It does not matter which world you choose; all must go through this. It is natural, it is the law, the eternal law. You must also feel pity for those Souls who do harm to others, who go through the good times for their own pleasure and do not learn within their lifetime. For these are the souls who wish to remain in the dark. This is when most of the work we as Spirit carry out. For there are many unenlightened souls who do not wish to open their hearts to anyone. They live in abject misery, for whilst they are in the dark and cannot see the light, they cannot find the things to make the light, so they will fumble about in the dark. These souls go to the Winterlands.

Please give others the understanding now which they need. Please remember all flowers are beautiful if looked after in the right way. The flowers by the roadside are just as nice as the cultivated flowers within your gardens, for these flowers grow through great hardships, but they still manage to blossom, and they still manage to give off a rich scent. Not all flowers come from the same seed, there is a rich variety, the same as the souls within your world. The most beautiful souls from your world are the ones who have lived through abject misery and survived and wish to help others whose actions are like a drop in the ocean.

12: Passing Over Before Your Chosen Time

As I have said earlier, the physical body has its own time of passing, do not hasten that time. Your mind and your body work as one, we have said many times, you are mind, body and spirit. Your body can be divided into seven, your mind can be divided into seven and you have seven spiritual bodies. If you pass before the time, you lose one of your spiritual bodies before the time is right. You must lose one veil from your mind, one spiritual body and one soul.

The reason being that if you lose any one prematurely, there is an imbalance, this makes the work harder for you. Many times, we see people brought over into the world of spiritual by means of your mechanical world, by your machines, and people also take their own lives. This is not right; this is not the natural law of the Spiritual World. These people, because of their imbalance, crave still for things on the physical world, but they cannot attain those things.

It is a sad time when someone passes through no fault of their own and to suffer this way. However, the things of the Spiritual World and the things of the Physical World should run as one, but the blind and the deaf do not realise these things. If you take a thing and move it out of its' natural world or its natural environment, then you'll have that blame on you. There is a story in your world where someone took the rabbit animal to another land, then they were overrun by that animal in that other land, and they ask the question if they should kill that animal, because that animal has become in their eyes a vermin, a pest. Man made that problem; man should stand up to that problem. You made the machines in your life; you make the wars in your world. Do not blame the Spirit World when people are taken in their youth, or when people are taken through these machines, or when people take their own lives through worries which at the time they cannot bear. You do not take on your shoulders any more than you can bear.

The machines of the physical world are made of the physical world. It is wrong for us to tell you how to run your lives in the physical world, though it is wrong for you to take the lives of each other. It is up to the people in the physical world who are down the path of enlightenment to bring about a knowledge of learning. The simple things in life are the best things in life. Less material gain, less material worries, less of the emotions in your world you call lust all lead to less emotional upset in your world. We have said these emotions are inward looking, we have said that the unenlightened in your world dwell too much on the physical pleasures. They have lost their way.

Questioner: "What happens when you do pass into the other life before your allotted time?"

Khan: "There are various forms. There are those which leave this world, by accident caused through your machines. Each one should have a natural time of passing, if this passing occurs consciously- if you are in pain, you will reach a state where the pain ceases to be.

You see your physical surroundings, but you see them more intensely, you see the brightness for as you die, as you call it, you are changing your vibration, your bodily vibrations. Your mind vibrates at a certain level, as you pass from one level to another, then the vibrations of your mind will speed, so you will see your physical life, your surroundings, you will see the colours, you will also feel the colours. Everything will

29

be enhanced. But slowly, it will begin to fade. You will then also hear music; it is the music of transition. You are crossing the boundaries to another realm, soon you will begin to hear music, you also begin to see vaguely at first, friends and relatives who have made the crossing before you. The physical realm will slowly fade, and your next world will begin to glow until you see clear.

The next world is dreamlike, for you have not yet left the physical self. If you have reached your natural time of passing, then you just wake up into the next world. Next, if it is the first passing or, it is not your natural time, then, you will feel confused and you will not hear the welcoming music but you will see your world more clearly the same, but you will find yourself incapable of communicating with those around you. You will not recognise those of the physical world and those of the spiritual world, it will seem like a dream. This is why it is important to be aware of where you go before this time approaches, for you will recognise with full knowledge where you have to go, but you will be in the 'in-between' world between the physical and the purely spiritual world.

You will find yourself in the darkness, you will be welcomed there by someone who has been allotted to you, who has been close to you spiritually and physically. And these will take care of you until you understand more of where you are.

All must go through this 'in-between' world. But you can arrive there on your own accord if this is your natural time. But if you have not reached your natural time, it is a false passing, then you will find yourself in this. These are which you call 'lost souls', it is an important part of our work, and sometimes they refuse to accept where they are and that they have passed over on to our side and they return to the earth themselves as they have material attachments and do not want to leave the physical world."

Questioner: "How does one know that it is an actual time to pass?"

Khan: "You would experience the difference. There could be a calmer passing, it is a normal drift from your world to ours. You will hear accompanying music, you will see the next world superimposed on yours, until your world disappears, and you find yourself in the spiritual world.

To have pain when passing, is not a natural passing. A natural passing is when before you entered your physical world you have a determined number of years within your world, when you have fulfilled this number then you drift into ours. There is a saying within your world that "you only have so many breaths to breath within your life." And by creating anger within yourself you are encouraging yourself to take more breaths, so you are shortening your life through anger. If you all led a calm life, if you all ate correctly, if you all did what should be termed as natural, then you would all live your full term. You all have the capacity for healing. Disease within your world can be healed, disease within your world should not be. There is no reason for disease."

Questioner: "Can you explain about people that pass when they are young and young innocent souls such as babies with disease or cot deaths?"

Khan: "To some people in your world, it may seem unfair to you. When babies die, when souls pass through disease, these souls are more developed souls than yours, these souls need less, these souls do not need as much teaching, they have learnt their lessons, they are on the earth plane for a little period because their learning is of a limited period so in affect it is their karma.

The longer you live on the earth plane, the more worries on your shoulders means that you are not developed enough, when your soul is at the right stage of development your time of passing will come. You determine the length before you enter the physical world. You determine the exams."

31

13: The Summer lands

There is a natural time for all of you to pass between the worlds. There should no longer be a need for the Summerland's. But in your natural time, when you have learnt the lessons which you chose to learn within this life, you will feel the need to pass to your next life. This need is deeply rooted within you, you will know when your natural time has come. When you pass between the worlds, it is the simplest thing. It is a release of all heaviness. It is a release of all concern and worry and your spirit will flow to the next world which some within your world call "the Summerland's". It is not the true spiritual world; it has many physical attributes. It is a place of learning. You have heard of the "Halls of Learning"? This resides within the Summerland's.

It is a place of learning, where you learn how to live within the spiritual world. Evermore increasing within your world, is the need for the Summerland. For you bring about a shortening of natural life from your inventions. And your ways of living which are unnatural to the machines which you call cars, they cause many deaths within your world which are unnecessary, so a soul may find itself in the spirit world sooner than it thought, so it needs to learn, it needs to get over the shock, for it is a shock when a soul passes unnaturally.

You all have a natural time. If you take your own lives or if you take the lives of others, whether it be accidental or premeditated, it is a shock to the soul. So, this soul must learn about the spiritual worlds, this is where the spiritual hospitals reside. As you would call them. They are not like hospitals within your world. You learn to live the spiritual life and unless you have learnt this you will not pass to the first of the spiritual kingdoms. In this you will be able to see things more clearly, you will be able to see the work which you have chosen, you will be able to see the design of the plan of things, still in a limited fashion, but you will be able to see the image of the truth which you have striven for all your lives. And you will find it necessary to judge and assess yourself. There are no souls within this world who are going to judge you, for you are master of your own lives.

No other soul can control you. It is wrong to lead others down paths which are not rightly theirs. So, you judge your own life, you assess the things which you have learnt and the things which you have not learnt, so you come to memories of things of which you have learnt in previous lives. You amass these things and you judge these things with the life which you have just vacated in the physical world. When you have amassed this knowledge within yourself and you have judged yourself, then it will be the true light of love and understanding. Then you pass for a second time. You will pass to the second of your spiritual kingdoms, which is of a finer and more subtle nature.

You will not understand the nature of this world yet, in this realm you will learn your lessons on the spiritual way, and it is a time of waiting for the rest of your Soul Group. Within this world you meet, and you recognise your Soul Group, and there you will judge again the things which you have learnt, but you judge these things within your Soul Group. You judge things fairly; you do not judge individuals. You are just and you judge the collective knowledge that you have gained, the interaction between each of you within the physical world and the interaction between yourself and others within the physical world. You may feel the need after this judgement for further lives within the physical world. You may feel the need to have others within the physical world, but for you to remain within the spiritual realms.

Many choose this option, or you may choose to go to the third kingdom, but if you are not ready for this kingdom you will be brought back to the physical world. The third kingdom is of a much finer nature. You can only visit this kingdom, this realm, when you are ready. For as you cannot join fire and water, you cannot join the third kingdom with yourselves until you are of that nature. You learn that you need to refine yourself more to fitting into this realm. There are many options open to you in the second realm. You may choose to have experiences in other realms or other worlds. There are many of those with life, all striving for the same as you, there are many worlds of a highly developed nature, of a more highly spiritual nature within your own role, within your own experiences.

Questioner: "When we pass over do, we retain a physical body?"

Khan: "You have a physical body for as long as you feel you need them. When you realise that you are truly of a spiritual nature, when you realise that the things which you hold dear within the physical world, no longer apply to the spiritual world, then you will see there is no need for your physical body. There is no need to look like you did within the physical world, you will recognise other souls from a feeling and from the love which that soul shows. You are all striving to become part of that cosmic life which is all around you from which you came and from which you will return, which all your teachers have taught you about

14: Health

When you are unwell or in time of need you must be aware of Spirit around you. You must connect with Spirit. You all have your own ways; you all have your own paths to tread. These paths are of your choosing. You have decided these paths before you entered the Physical World.

Mental problems and problems of the Spirit can be resolved by looking into your own hearts. Physical problems are of a different nature. Physical problems come about through your living. They come through your lifestyles, and they come through your backgrounds. You must learn to live simple lives; your needs must be very basic. These are hard lessons. These are lessons which have been taught through the ages, but through these lessons come benefits, great benefits. You will be at ease with yourselves, you will be at ease with each other, and you will feel a great spirit from the earth nature. We know the pressures of your living. We know the pressures of your world. We sympathise, we come from an earlier time when our lives were simpler. If we did need greater lessons to learn we would have chosen your world. Only the strong come to your world. You must always remember your past lives; always remember this is the life of your choosing. You must find strength in that choice, for in that choice you show to yourself that you are willing to go through more to gain the lessons and to gain your home, the celestial light. We all are, and we all go from the same. You must feel infinity with each other and the animal kingdom. The simpler your lives the less stress and worry.

 Questioner: "Why do we get disease?" Khan: "Because of the way in which you, or your fellow man decide to live. With some there is no choice. Because it is passed to them from others. Disease has to start somewhere, disease is dis-ease. The way to cure the disease is by giving of yourself, also pass understanding to help the underdeveloped to understand that basics of life, cleanliness of mind and body.

Within your world, the innocent catches these diseases. You must cure the diseases, you must cure the diseases from source, it does not mean to say that if a child dies from disease, that it was born with disease, or if it was born with disease, the disease that exists within that body itself has grown within your world. You are not born with disease, you acquire disease." Questioner: "Some babies are born with disease." Khan: "Because of the source within your world, if you all live correctly, there will be no disease within your world."

Questioner: "How do you in turn live correctly?"

Khan: "By eating correctly, by looking after yourself correctly."

Questioner: "If that is not available, what do you do then?"

Khan: "Also, hygiene. You are thinking only of your immediate surroundings, you must think of your place of birth as the earth itself, the diseases start from underdeveloped countries, and they go through a long progression and they evolve within themselves to the disease until it affects a great many. There is sufficient food within your world for all, there is sufficient medicines in your world for all."

Questioner: "They don't all cure."

Khan: "There should be no need to starve within your world, there should be no need for disease within your world."

Questioner: "How about cancer?"

Khan: "Cancer is a cell that breaks, and it effects the cells around it to die, because you have as you term it,' evolved into a certain thing. Cancer does not always correct itself, if you look at the Eskimo, the Eskimo up to normal times did not suffer with heart diseases it did not suffer cancers at all.

It is all through contact with the so called civilised that they contracted these diseases. It just shows you that it is not natural for you to have these diseases. You can fight them. If you use your mind correctly, then you would not be bothered by disease, by improving you mind."

Questioner: "By meditation you mean?"

Khan: "By meditation or by whatever you have. It is not easy, you must have purity of mind, or simplicity of mind."

Questioner: "Some religions are saying that AIDS and other illnesses are Gods intervention What is Spirits view on this?

What you are asking is, are we intervening in your lives? We have said many times, the way of the physical world we cannot rule. We cannot make our lives manifest in your world, unless we are reborn. The diseases of your world are physical, so therefore, it follows that the diseases of your world are made by a physical nature and are made by physical beings. It is not divine intervention!"

15: Living the Path

All men are looking for something. You have books in your world from the Jesus Master and the followers of the Jesus Master. There is one book called the Book of James, from your Bible. In this book it talks about questions and it talks about the attitude. Like I have said we cannot rule your life. You have chosen your life. The path you tread is of your own making. The laws of our world; the world of Spirit, also apply to your world. You have heard of the Law of Karma. The life you lead is of your own making.

The Spirit James tells you this. In this book you have no need to read between the lines, it is there for all to read. If you are of the physical nature and you have not that spiritual knowledge, you will read in a different way from the spiritually minded. That is why there are so many churches and so many beliefs in your world. People use the spiritual knowledge which they have gained for their own use, and for their own gain. This is not the way of the Spirit World; therefore they will not progress, this is why it is easy to find flaws in their teachings.

In all teachings there is truth. Whether there is a truth of the physical world or the truth of the spiritual world. The word truth in your world has its roots in the Hebrew meaning, its roots mean 'to lean on' and 'to use; that is why it is important to question. You take the questions and answers to your hearts. If you can use them in your world, if you can use them for the furthering of others, or for the furtherance of Spirit teachings, or even for making your life easier, then this truth has proven itself. You can lean on this truth and you can use this truth to the benefit of yourself and of others. That is why you must ask. If the answers do not satisfy you, ask more questions. If you do not understand, ask more questions. We want whole minds and whole bodies; a divided mind is of no use, neither in your world nor our world because a divided mind will always be questioning itself and it will always be working against itself, so we need whole minds, we need clear minds.

Through asking questions and gaining the truth, you gain the light. Your spiritual books talk about the teachings of the Father. We gave teachings in your ancient world for the time, at their level of understanding," that is why the teachings of the ancient world differ from the teachings now. The spiritually minded in your world are not persecuted, it is because understanding is now growing. So, when your books teach of the Father and of the God, the one God, it refers to the one Light and the teachings of Light. For the teachings of light hide no shadows. There are no shadows in the perfect light. If there are shadows in the light of the teachings, reject these.

If you cannot see clearly, then the teachings are false. If the teachings have their limitations, then the teachings are no good. Seek another Master; seek another teacher for all teachers should give you the different knowledge and the perfect light, with all understanding.

Once again in your books, in your Bible books, it teaches that you must set your own house in order. It is hard. All the physical problems pray on your mind. It is hard to remove these problems, but by living a simple life, and by using the teachings of Spirit in their purest form you can gain that knowledge. You can gain that peace. By gaining that peaceful home, that peaceful mind, you can set yourself at peace. If your mind is in torment, it is hard. It is the path that you have chosen, it is the life you have chosen to lead. Your life is a result of your living. We do not mean to sound harsh, we do not like to look down on you and judge, for we cannot judge you. Only you can judge yourself. You must judge yourself; you must look at yourself, you must look inwardly. You must look towards your heart. If you have a Heart centre which is bigger than your other Centres, (see chapter Chakras, Colour and Healing) this is wrong. You must work on your other centres. You must bring into your Centres a balance. You must bring into your life a balance, and you must use Spirit with a balance. We would dearly love to slip into your lives to set your world straight, but only you can judge, only you can change your way. We are sorry, but you have chosen your life. You have chosen your life to suit your nature and your lessons. Be a strong person and do not be weak in your life. You must think about this and you must gain courage from this. In your moments of weakness, you gain strength. In your moments of strength, you gain weakness. You must set a balance.

16: Same Gender Relationships

Q*uestioner*: "At one time the Church, and many people even now, are of the attitude that this is wrong. What is the view from Spirit on this?"

Khan: "We have said each soul chooses its own life. Each should have its own road to travel down. They show love. Is it wrong to show love? It is not wrong to love one another, in whatever form. These people start with the lower Chakra centres, but often it progresses into a natural love relationship. It is love of the heart. This is not wrong. We must not ostracize people for their beliefs. These dogmas and the teachings of your society. Unless they are good teachings. Unless they can be proven. Unless they can benefit the heart. They are wrong.

Within the Bible there are which says that you must love your fellow man. He does not state which sex, yet you must love. It also states you must not love your own sex. This was the safeguard of the people of the time, for it was shown in your world through your living. It brings about problems. The people who you call 'Gay' have their own problems. You are currently suffering in your world the disease of these union (AIDS), which is why in your Bible, it states that it is wrong.

They also say in your Bible that it is right to take more than one wife, yet in your own society it is wrong.

In order to safeguard the people in the ancient times, we gave guidelines and teachings up to their knowledge, up to their spiritual knowledge and their mental knowledge. For if you ate meat which was off, it would kill, the people in the ancient times were not to eat meat - a specific type of meat or they caught diseases. They were not permitted to drink or eat blood, for these brought about diseases, but in your world, you have the knowledge and understanding to overcome these diseases. So, it is up to your own level of understanding and teachings, up your own societies to deal with these problems.

It is wrong to make game of these teachings. It is wrong to subdue others from teachings whether from a physical nature or a spiritual nature. From your birth you are taught many things. You are taught to respect your elders and not to respect your enemies - your enemies are also your elders. You are taught from birth about love, about family love, but you are taught it is wrong to love others.

We are all souls of equal rights; you must look at each individual soul within your world as you would a stained-glass window. It is pointless looking at these windows at night, you must only look at these windows when the sun is shining through them. You can see all the colours, you can see all the pattern, you can see the beauty and the craftsmanship which has gone into making that window. You can see the soul of that window. Never look at anyone in any lesser light that you would look at yourselves.

You must love all, you must shake the cloak off your societies. You must shake off your cloak of your religious dogmas.

These religions served at the time; the times have now changed. But through the many: many others will seek the light.   Things   will   slowly   change."

17: Previous Lives

You must remember your past and your future. Each one of you should remember your past and your previous lives. Ask the child. The child knows, the child's mind is not cluttered with doctrines and dogmas. You must strip away your religions, you must see things in a new light, you must try and see the colours. You must look at the world and study the world, for in the world is a great insight into your spiritual being. You must strip away the fears of life, they hinder, they contract. There is only one look and emotion, which is love. You cannot expand your consciousness; you can expand love. All things feed off love, all things need love, the animal world responds to love.

Even in the physical world there is wisdom. It is no accident that between the physical world and our world is a two-way communication. We try to impart wisdom and knowledge and we also learn once more to be a part of your world. We know there are a great many questions which you will ask. You cannot ask questions without the knowledge, so by asking your questions, is one way to evaluate your progression. There have been a great many worries about the problems in your world. Many people say, 'Why do the good die young?' 'Why does the hard-working die young?'

You should all know the answers, my children. You should be able to investigate your previous lives and your existences and see your development. For did not each of you elect to be born again in the physical world. You took upon yourselves your own worries; the spirit will not give worries to anyone unable to carry them. It is all a learning process; of the things you haven't learnt or have neglected to hear in previous lives.

In the First Kingdom you take on the lessons you have not learnt. In the Second Kingdom, after you have judged yourselves, you take on the lessons for your next lives.

You should be able to remember these somewhere along the path of enlightenment.

You live your life according to your previous lives, for in each life you learn something different. By recalling previous lives, you can avoid making the same mistakes again, by dwelling on the unpleasant side of your reincarnations. In these lessons you have experienced many things, many different cultures, and many different creeds. Your past lives have all been centred around certain religions and philosophies. You take medicine within the physical world. You know the medicine will taste not very nice, but you still must take that medicine. So, you gulp it down and forget it, but the memory is still there. You know you must learn certain things; you will remember the bad as well as the good!

From the memories you always look for the good ones, but you must remember the bad ones for these are the lessons which you chose to go through. Each time you manifest in a different experience, you will feel a bond with other members of your soul group, you each of you go through these experiences together, in these past lives you will meet many people, but you stay closest to the people of your soul group, because you carry these memories and these experiences over with you into other lives, you will attract Guides and Helpers of these experiences.

It is hard, your minds are clouded with the dogmas of others, but you must look into their souls. You must question. Even question the words of Spirit. You must ask other teachers of our world imparting the knowledge to you for your own ends; is it a genuine need to help the physical world? You must also look at the teachers in your own world and you must judge their souls, how they are teaching. For their own egos or is it a genuine need to help others? You must also look at all teachings and question them. If you can find a logical path, if you can ask questions and be told answers, it is the right path. So many teachers say, "you must believe and have faith, you must not ask questions, but have faith." How can you develop if not by asking questions? How can you see the way home without seeing the path to tread?

These things are important. You must question, you must ask. Only by asking can you evaluate your own progression, only by asking questions can you see the way home.

We don't make things into mysteries; we try to make things clear. Only by making things clear can you see through them, can you see the knowledge, can you see the work.

The scientific world and the spiritual world have for so long been at war. Things now are beginning to be explained by your scientific leaders. Many people in the field of science are coming to a knowledge of the spiritual worlds but there are still a lot of questions, a lot of work to be done. Do not be discouraged when each question you ask ten more develop. This is the way of things. Have we not said 'the seed can only develop in the appropriate soil? You are enriching your own soil, so that you can accept a deeper spirit. A deeper seed is planted to cultivate your souls and your heart. This you already know, in your quiet times when you feel lonely. Feel your left hand with your right, this is how close we are. We try to be your right hand.

The lives which you live are fast lives, you do not have time for yourselves. That which remains still is easiest to hold. That which is fast moving is very difficult to hold, you must slow your lives down. You must lead simple lives. Simple lives bring simple problems. All joys are based on hatred, all happiness is based on misery. There is a light side and there is a dark side. You must realise this; you must slow your lives down and hold on to that which you find dear. It is hard to see your individual journeys, to walk a thousand miles it starts with the ground beneath your feet. Do not look at the present, look at the future which may be. There is a goal behind every action. You must realise it is your life and nobody else's. You must walk your own pathways, you must overcome your own troubles, for you bring these about. The degree of trouble depends on the degree of life which you live. You must walk your own path, do not look for the easy ways. Do not ride somebody else's car to get to your destination for you have to travel roads which have been made by others. You must travel your own pathway, use and make your own pathway. Do not look for the easy options for the easy options are for others. Do not walk somebody else's road. Is this understandable? To learn to be happy you must first be unhappy. To learn to be truly joyous you must learn abject misery. You must experience all things to find that which you seek, otherwise you are not leading a true life, you are not leading a true existence. This is one of the reasons why you abide within the physical world, to learn and to watch. You must see without seeing, and you must feel without pain. You must feel your way through life. You must not judge others. If they judge you, this is their own pathway. You must be not with words but with actions.

There is much spoken about non-action. Through non-action you gain action. Without speaking you give the impression of a thousand words thorough your actions. You must lead a still life. You must lead a simple life. Do not underestimate your own karmic destinies, for whatever you desire, you will receive. So, make your desires of a simple nature, then what you receive will be understandable. It is easy to grasp new ideas from an early stage it is hard to encompass the whole of things; you must start slowly. You do not plant fully grown trees within your gardens, this would be impractical. You must start with a seed, but you must also learn that not every flower comes from the same seed. There are many different seeds and it is up to you to find which seed is suitable for the souls within your world. You must be able to look at other souls in a righteous way without judgement and find what that soul needs. Every soul has a different   need.

18: Spirit World Judgement and Morals

When you pass from this world you will gain the kingdom which I think you call the Summer lands. Here you will learn about the spirit world. You will learn to leave behind the attributes of the physical world. Your feelings will alter as you learn that you gain your kingdom. You will see that the things you learnt in the physical world are of no use to you. Therefore, you do not need your physical world values, for you will gain moral values of a different nature.

When you have passed, you judge yourself and you pass again and re-join your Soul Group. Then you assess what you have learnt collectively, if you feel you have not learnt enough to go to the Third Kingdom, you will then reincarnate, but it does not have to be in this form.

When you judge yourself for the next kingdom, you judge yourself without bias in the pure light of love. There are no such things as morals, these are of an earthly nature. Man-made rules are for the physical world.

It is moral guilt within your world that says that you can only love one person. Is this not right? In the spirit world, you will learn to love everybody. Why merit yourselves with rules and regulations which mean nothing? Your world is a very limited world, very limited in understanding. It is good to have rules to be a good person, but you should not need rules to be a good person. Therefore, you should not need moral values, for you should know what is right and what is wrong. You do not need any rules to tell you. Is this not so? There is only one rule and that is love. If you have that within yourself, then you do not need rules or regulations for you treat everybody how you would wish yourself to be treated. You only make rules and regulations when people do not live accordingly. Do the flowers make rules and regulations to enable them to grow? Does the sun have to have rules and regulations to shine? This is how you must look at your world. Therefore, we give you the symbols of the garden. For every right action, every right path a flower will grow in your own special garden until your garden is full. Then it is time to go for the third kingdom. You are living your lives in a physical world to enable you to build your garden, a garden of the heart. You must cultivate your heart; you must let it sing.

19: Transplants

The soul who called himself White Eagle and the soul who called Silver Birch. Both said the same: that it is wrong to transplant from one soul to another, for within each soul, within each cell, there is a personality of that soul. It is wrong to mix these. There is a natural time of passing. Before you enter this world, you decide on how long you wish to live in that world. It is wrong to try to make a soul live longer than its allotted time. We work along Scientists and Doctors. We try to help souls whose time have been shortened through actions from your world, we have said before there is a natural time of passing. Many souls within your world pass well before their time through mis-action, through the so-called vehicles of your world, through the hatred of your world, through wars. These are not natural times of passing. We do not judge you if you make the decision to give part of your body as transplant or have a transplant.

You must gain the balance within yourselves; you must live with what is right for you and what is wrong for you. It is wrong for us to tell you to do or not to do. But we say there is an allotted time. Why not try to stop the wars? Why not try to stop the accidents through thoughtlessness which happen in your world; Then we would not need the transplants, if you all lived accordingly and not fouled your bodies with the things that you eat, with things which you take into your body, you would not need this.

20: The Garden and Flowers

D o you understand about the garden? The garden is symbolic of how each of you should be. There are many things in a garden which makes up the collective beauty. There are many different species. There are many different colours, many different scents, but they all make up the one garden. You cannot have one flower. We call it a garden. You need many varieties, many different scents, to make up the garden. Build your own foundations, for you plan your gardens. You do not just go into your garden and plant the plants anywhere they happen to be. You plan your garden to have pleasant effects, for you wish for beauty. You do not wish for chaos. So, you must plan your lives in the same manner as you would plant your gardens.

This is how your life should be. You must take the garden as symbolic. You take the strength from the trees; the trees can withstand many things. The winds of change may blow, but the trees still bear fruit. You take great delight in the scents and the many different colours of the flowers. You take a greater understanding of life itself through watching the interaction of the insects and the flowers. Each one depends on the other.

A tree cannot bear fruit without the insects. It is symbolic of how your life should be. You must look at all things and see the importance of all things. You cannot live your life by yourself, you are dependent on influences around you. These influences may alter your state of being which will alter your attitude which in the long run will alter your pathways. You must pick out these influences like you would pick out your favourite flowers. If it brings delight and happiness, then it is a good attitude. Just as you would not look at an ugly form to give you pleasure, you all have your own favourite flowers. This is no accident. You must look at the relation between all. You must look at the relation of action and non-action, for many things can be gained through action, through the correct action. Many things can be gained through the state of non-action and non-being. To explain: You have the window, a window cannot be without the space. This is action and non-action, the solid and the invisible. There is a time of doing and there is a time of non-doing, you must learn the balance within your lives in all things.

21: The Seven Levels of Consciousness

There are seven levels of consciousness, which some call the Astral World, which some call Heaven. You have heard of the saying 'seventh heaven', these heavens reside within each of you. They are obtainable by yourself. There are seven spiritual bodies, each one resides on its level of consciousness or its own level in the astral worlds. Spiritual development means that you will gain a knowledge of your higher self which resides in the next world, which is an integral part of you, which is part of you and once you understand and you can be in touch with your next spiritual self, then you will be on a further understanding and you will be able to reach deeper within yourself and gain your next spiritual consciousness or self. You do not have to go elsewhere to find these heavens or these other selves, for they all reside within each of you. Heaven is not above you or below you, it is within each of you. You have heard of the macrocosm and the Microcosm. Within each of you is the Microcosm which is endless. There is a greater world without you and there is a greater world or worlds within you. What is without is within. Does this make it plain? There is a universe all around you, there is a universe within you, this is the Macrocosm and the Microcosm. They cannot exist without each other.

There is a physical state of being and there is a mental or spiritual state of being. You will pass eventually from the physical state of being and you will learn to develop yourself within the spiritual worlds. The physical world is the macrocosm and the spiritual worlds is the microcosm. You will gain an understanding of these through reaching within yourselves, for you are all on the pathways which you elected, and we are pleased that these pathways are of a good and wholesome nature. As it has been proved many of you are beginning to understand that seed. You cannot gain a knowledge of your higher self without this understanding. You cannot look for an object in a dark room without the light of knowledge, otherwise you stumble around in the dark without knowing where to look, so you must have the pure light of knowledge. This will illuminate your pathway and your search. We do not ask you to understand everything, you must take things in small steps. Moderation of things brings great success. You need nourishment for your bodies to live. Too much nourishment for your body will alter the structure of your body and bring about chemical changes which are undesirable in your body. So, moderation in all things will bring great success. Take small steps. Take firm steps, for, as the quotation goes, 'The longest journey starts with but a single step'. Is this not true?

When you find the balance within yourself, you will not conflict with the things which surround you. A wheel cannot be a wheel unless it is round, unless all sides are even, otherwise even the shortest of journeys will be the most uncomfortable of journeys. Do you understand? So, make your first steps short steps, and build your own foundations. Therefore, we give the garden as a symbol.

22: The Astral World

The Astral World is an 'in-between' world. The Astral World lies between our world and the First Kingdom. The earth plane is of a denser heavier vibration but as we climb higher towards the higher vibrations from each lifetime, the vibration is a lot finer.

The Astral World is where a Soul learns that they are no longer on the earth plane. They learn how to be in the Spirit World. They visit the Summerland's and learn about past lives and go to their library. In the Astral World they have hospitals as we understand them and each soul that passes over that needs healing will be there until their understanding grows about the Astral World and how they live within that world. They also heal themselves with the help of their chosen Guide who has been close to them in their previous life or lives They stay there until they are ready to go and join their Soul Group and collectively decide if they have learnt what they had chosen to learn and move to a higher plane of existence or come back to the earth world and reincarnate.

23: Astral Projection

When we asleep, our Inner self or Soul or Spirit can leave the body and move between the levels of existence. It is a natural thing we do. Some people call it Astral Projection. To describe the sensation that we feel it is like being a deep-sea diver at the bottom of the deepest ocean. At the bottom we need special suits to be able to live there, but as you move up through the levels you need fewer heavy suits and it gets lighter and it is less dense. For those that can remember their out of body experiences they will always say the next level is so light and not as dense as this level that we reside in.

We are not physical beings but deep inside us (or the Divers Suit) is the true us, a spiritual being. As we evolve, we move from one existence to another. We move toward the light moving forever upward through the levels. We leave our suits or 'overcoats' (physical bodies) behind when we move on to the next level because the next level is more of a finer vibration. We do not need our physical body. The next level is a world of thought and pure energy It is a finer vibration. We do not need our physical bodies.

One person who shared their experience of leaving their body behind said that they saw 'Thought Shells' on the next level. The thought shells looked like glass containers in human form. These forms are left behind when the physical bodies are shed and have moved on to their next level of existence. The shells slowly decay.

When it is our time to leave this physical existence and evolve, we leave our human forms behind.

24: Astral Projection: Out of Body Experiences

"It was in 1985. I read an article in a well-known magazine on Astral Projection and how to achieve the experience. I originally thought it was a way of making lucid dreams. I followed the system written in the article. I tried this system for quite a long time and tried to fall asleep with my conscious mind but each time I would fall asleep and remember nothing of any dream that I had.

One Sunday morning after working a long shift at work I could not sleep as was overly tired. But at about 2.15am just before I fell asleep, I heard a loud crash in my head, and I felt myself flying down a black tunnel towards a multi coloured light. There was music coming from everywhere. I felt it coming from myself. I was the music too; I was engulfed in it.

I then noticed I was being pulled down a tunnel by two monks one on either side of me, holding each arm. I felt as if there were hundreds of eyes watching me. I felt a warm gentle breeze on my face. I was being led towards a light at the end of the tunnel and as I went through it, I slowly drifted down to a black and white tiled floor. At this time, I knew I was not dreaming because I felt the cold tiled floor when I touched down. The area was all bathed in white light.

I couldn't see any walls. The tiles on the ground to my left and right disappeared into the distance. About 20 or so feet Infront of me there was a table, but it also stretched into the distance and behind that I saw hundreds of people all dressed in white. Some of them came towards the table and I recognized some of them as family that had passed over. I do feel that I should have known them all. I am sure they were relatives. One came right up to me and it was my Grandad who had passed over when I was a boy. He came up to me and said 'What are you doing here? It's not your time yet.' I got emotional and because of a thought entering my head I shot back into my body.

When I looked at the clock it was only 2.16am. I had been away just One minute!"

I knew it was not a dream for when you have an Out of Body experience the next level is not as dense as the level here on earth. It is more real than this life. Once you have had an experience then it does get easier every time you do it." Another experience I had...

... Again, I was taken through the tunnel. But this time found myself floating above my body getting closer to the ceiling. I expected to bump my head but instead I found myself passing through the ceiling to the other side, but instead of the loft I was laying on grass.

When I sat up every blade of grass was so green, and I could see everything so clearly. It was as if my eyesight was Ultra HD. Once again, the grass extended well into the horizon. The sky was so blue. The temperature was not hot or cold, but just perfect. It is hard to explain.

There was just one tree on the horizon, a big oak tree. I felt I wanted to get closer and didn't quite know how to get there. There was a voice in my head that said, 'turn yourself into an eagle and fly to the tree'. I felt someone behind me and there stood a North American Indian, who just smiled at me. He radiated a glow, a slight golden light. He felt a beautiful Spirit. I then felt myself jump upward and stretched my arms out and I was flying. I know how things might sound but I changed into an eagle. The feeling of the wind over my feathers and knowing what a bird feels as it is flying will never leave me. I got to the oak tree and I tilted my wings and my legs pushed forward to grab a branch. For that moment I had all the instincts of a bird. Again, I put a thought in my head about the experience and I was back in my bed! Each time that I have been spoken to in the Astral World I have heard it in my head. It is hard to explain the feeling of being there. The colours are so vivid, vibrant. There is a sound that comes from the trees, grass, the wind. Everything together which when put together makes beautiful music. You realise it is all part of the whole. I imagine it is about vibration. We are all part of the same song. 'The Song of Life'. At this time of having these experiences I thought that Astral Projection was a way of having lucid dreams and not real, but they had such an impact on me they were the most life changing events of my life. One day I was reading a book on the subject and spoke to a colleague at work about it. This colleague had learning difficulties as he had been a forceps baby. He asked me what Astral Projection was and I explained it to him and to my surprise he said, 'Oh that, I do that all the time'. The Doctors' had told him that he was brain damaged, so I did not take much notice but then he said that he would come to my house in his 'other body' as he called it.

He had never been to my house and he lived some distance away from me, so I said okay I will leave old electric cards out around the house and I will draw symbols on them. Not really believing that he could do that. That night, I drew symbols on the cards and put the cards out around the house and went to bed and forgot all about it.

The following day at work. He not only told me about the symbols on the cards (I had placed six cards around the house) but the places where I left them. He also told me how each room was decorated, and what clothes were in the bathroom floor, and who slept in each room.

Another time I found myself in a cave which led to two tunnels, one on the left which had a yellow light emanating from it and one on the right which had a green light. I took the right-hand tunnel. I didn't have such a wonderful experience from this one.

The following day my colleague came up to me and said "I noticed you went to the left-hand tunnel. I saw you. Next time take the right-hand tunnel you will have a much more pleasant experience."

This really convinced me about his 'other body' journey." And that my experiences were real. There is still so much to learn about ourselves and the many levels that exist."

25: Life Before Life

Before your spirit body meets with its' Soul Group, your Spirit Body is in a primitive form of evolution. You have heard of the phrase "New Souls", these souls do not just appear. These souls have experienced previous forms of existence. It is no accident that you take care of the animals, that you love the animals. The more developed you become the more sensitive you are. The reason for this is because your spiritual body has inhabited the animal form, then you develop from the animal form to become a new soul.

Questioner: "So, we as 'new souls' emerged as animals and then were born as humans?"

Khan: All things have a natural progression."

Questioner: "I personally do not agree with that. How does that transpire that we started as animals?"

Khan: "Can you explain to me where new souls arrive form?"

Questioner: "I presume from the light as far as I understand. I do not know."

Khan:" then where do animals come from?"

Questioner: "From the light?"

Khan: "They all come from the light, why is there division within the light? So, animals come from the light."

Questioner: "I believe that animals are just as intelligent as we are, so why do we have to start from there and work up. Sometimes people are not as intelligent as animals."

Khan: "It is the natural way; you have to experience all!"

Questioner: "So, what you are actually saying is that we have all been animals?" Khan: "There are seven levels within each of the seven levels. Also, there are many souls within your world that all say this, they say that you return to the light. There is only one spark of intelligence, all spark of life which is the same as plants, trees, animals or yourself. Life cannot be divided into sections, life is. Life will be. Your life that is within you..., the life that is within you is the same as that is within animals, it is the same that is within the trees, the physical self will differ, but the life itself is spirit. It is the same."

Questioner: "How about plants then, does that mean that we have been plants as well?"

Khan: "It is so" ...

Questioner: "So we started from plants?"

Khan: "No! We started before. You start from the smallest things that there is before you start as plants. From the smallest cell then eventually progress to plants, then to animals then to humans."

Questioner: "Then you would think that the lives that we have had to live to get to the human form that people would be more understanding and empathic. People torture and abuse animals. They are then the same as us ... sentient beings that should be treated with compassion."

Khan: "You only have so many physical or uniform lives, you are attracted to certain animals. Have you ever felt empathy for the elephants? As a pet, the Indians used them for work.

You could choose any animal that you have an infinity with or towards. You may like certain animals more than others this is not because that you once were with them but also because you were also them. Can you imagine what it is like to hunt like a tiger? How can you know what it is like to hunt like a tiger if you have no knowledge of being so? You cannot imagine things which you have not experienced."

If you do not wish to understand this or to accept this, it is not important, you do not have to wish it if you do not want to.

Questioner: "I will admit that I find it very difficult to accept!"

Khan: "There will be many within your world who will be confused, or they will accept or disbelieve many things which I have said. This is the least of the controversial ideas. There are many more that you will find more of a struggle and hard to accept yourself.

As I have stated many times, you may accept or disbelieve if you wish. If there are terms or phrases or ideas within, that you feel they are of benefit or a comfort then this is good to only accept that, not to worry over things if you do not believe or accept.

I do not ask to be believed in all for all have their own truth, as there are many different diamonds each one is cut in a different way, and reflects a different light, but are all beautiful too.

Eating meat will bring karma to those that eat it in the future. Remember cause and effect. Every action has a reaction in life.

Remember the saying "Do unto others as you would have them do unto you!"

26: Music, Energy and Vibration

You all enjoy music. There are certain notes in music that put you in certain moods. There is a note responding to each power which also corresponds to each Chakra of light within your bodies. You are your lowest note of the seven, which vibrates at a slower level, which refers to your physical self, the base self (Red).

Each sound vibrates at a certain level. It affects you in certain ways, for you do not hear the sound, but it causes vibration, which you hear/feel. According to the level of vibrational sound this changes the moods which you are in.

You have the love of music, for you care about others. It is only natural to have music within you. There is a colour and a sound for each of your bodies. It is no accident in your history that certain religions or archaeological discoveries have held musical drawings or instruments.

In your cultures as far back as you could go there has always been musical thought. When light first appeared on this world, in the primitive way, you did not all talk. It was the sound which came first. It was the sound in you that came first. It is also no accident that the sound which you write first 'O' is the shape you can make with your mouth. You also sound the same shape. Also, if you measured the sound even from the vibration it would also make the same pattern. For you feel the vibration of the sound, you feel the vibration within you. This is how you reach your higher levels, through reaching out to each individual vibration around you. You understand, there is a vibration for each individual body. You master the vibration, the more spiritual or action you make. For there are no solid objects within your world.

If you compress all the physical compounds and all the matter that make up your body together, you would end up with only a handful of material. But what holds these compounds and particles together is the way that they attract and repel to vibration. They all vibrate at a certain level and there is a field around them which is caused through this vibration which you may call "electromagnetic energy," which is a force which is all around you and every living thing. You can use this energy if you are aware of the energy within you to detect impulses and energies around you, for they all interact. Everything is made up of energy and vibration. The whole of the universe could be compressed to less than the size of your room. The whole of the physical side of life. It makes up planets, stars and everything within your universe which may be compressed to the size of your room. Each individual body of matter is made up of particles. The particles are made up of atoms and there is an electromagnetic field which flows around each individual atom. Sometimes it may be positive, sometimes it may be negative. It changes at times; it is what repels and attracts. But each particle must vibrate, it must move at a certain level, at a certain pitch.

If you look at the notes that are in your own music, the lowest note refers to the material side of things. It is a slower vibration it vibrates at a lot slower pitch. The highest one - there are seven basic notes, within seven basic groups - this is one of your spiritual, semi spiritual and earthly bodies.

All your bodies vibrate at a different level. When you pass from your physical to your next level you pass the veil - you change vibration, the vibration which makes up you is higher or faster, as you wish. The higher up the evolutionary scale you go the nearer you get to your own inner self which is the seventh and last of your bodies. Each one is of a faster or higher rate than the previous one. But each has a specific colour as well. For does not light also travel in wave form. Waves travel through your air by vibration, also sound travels through vibration.

Sound and light are vibration ... they are one. Questioner: "Do the spirit people travel at the speed of light?

Khan: "They travel at their speed, of vibration."

Questioner: "What is the speed of thought?"

Khan: "The speed of thought is something which you will not be able to comprehend, you can comprehend the speed of light because it is a measurable thing from your side. It is a length of time, is it not, for we do not have time, we only have thought. We only have existence, we have no need of time, do you understand.

To understand thought, you must be of higher level or a higher vibration. But relate each note within your world, for everything revolves around seven. There are seven days of the week, seven colours, seven bodies, the colours and the bodies have the sound values also to each body, which are important. This is why you feel calm when a certain type of music is played. You feel aggressive when others are played.

I am being told that there is a piece of music which you know, which is to do with the planets, also this goes to prove power within your world and sound within your world.

There is one called Mars which is reputedly to be the god of war. The god of aggression. Mars is also the Red planet and the music which accompanies this idea is also of an oppressive nature. Then it puts the inner self on a lower level, does it not.

It gets you in an aggressive or an active mood. This is because colour ideology and sound come together to give you a prism, a thought. You understand. it is important to keep all together."

Questioner: "Why do they call Mars the planet of War, is it just a physical expression "

Khan: "You understand the moon that surrounds your own sphere, it has its own influence, to the invisible forces which are all around you, they manifest in many ways.

It alters the water levels on your world, does it not? It is also a sign of emotion. Those born under the sign of the moon are usually the people of an emotional nature. It manifests its influence in many ways. There is a term for this sphere 'Luna', and people of a deranged nature, the term called lunatics are more active under the influence of the full moon.

No matter how much you try to block out the influence from this sphere, animals, insects, mammals will always be affected at the times of the full moon. So, you see what influence this has upon your world. Each of those spheres that surround the sun all have their own field of influence. It is something which you should all be aware of.

There are seven basic spheres. For two of these spheres that surround your sun are too far removed to be effective to you, for there are also two more spheres which your world does not know about. They have not come across them yet. But the influence of the outer four are so weak as to be negligible within your world. So, there are seven basic spheres which all involve you. Does this explain? And the different configurations and positions of these spheres all make different influences.

You see? You are made of energy, you are not made of matter, you are energy, there are two basic things which are important in your own makeup that is water and energy. There are people within your world who call themselves "Dowsers", they claim to find water, they do not feel that actual water, some can see the water, others go on the feel of energy which water makes, they cannot feel influence from deep water, only from water when it flows against slower water. Shallow water or edges of riverbanks or underground streams, for the energy caused by water flowing over solid earth, they can feel, and they feel it because they are made of energy and water, themselves, you understand. So there are many forces and influences around you at all times which you must all be aware of, for if you are aware of all forces and influences, then you know what forces and influences there are around you to be used in your own way. Or if you do not know of a certain energy or force that is around you, then you cannot know how to use this. The power of thought is energy, it is a thing which is measurable within your world, your mind is capable of drawing together different types of energies, for each separate thought which you have is a different configuration of different energies of different particles of which all can be measured at different levels.

There are seven levels to the brain. Do you understand? Each level of thought is responsible for a different reaction. The first level of thought is bringing together basic energies around to pass information, not to receive information. The second level of thought is for rest and recuperation. It is drawing together energies that are needed to be replaced. The third level of consciousness is the level which you use to work out problems, and for an insight into your physical world and so on and so forth until you get to the spiritual level.

If someone laughs around you is it not contagious? Again, you feel the energy. You don't know why it is funny, but you start to laugh. This soul would vibrate at a certain level, these energies are felt around. And it would also influence the energies around you, and you would feel this. Why do you laugh when you do not know why? This is how you use certain energies and how you feel the energies.

Another example of this is football matches or mass gatherings. One person feels the anger and is then spread to others through and eventually we have a mass crowd hysteria...but there are more deep and practical energies also, that you must also be aware.

It is all simple, you do not have to know about the seven notes, the seven colours. The animal kingdom does not know, it is only because you have divorced yourselves from your own roots, from your own ancestral and spiritual knowledge which you all have within, through the way in which you lead your lives. Is this not so?

Is there not a trend in your world to go back to simpler things? To go back to the old ways, for the old ways seemed happier, seemed simpler. This is because of the old ways, there was also knowledge, there was also being "who you were".

You make life complicated; man did not have to use words to express ideas, he could impress them on the minds of others. He needed sound to explain what was around him, he used to make sound. Music first, then the pictures came then the speech, which only complicated things."

27: Mediumship

Q*uestioner*: "Mediums who are doing this work for Spirit, who give their lives to bring understanding about the spirit world. Who bring loved ones who have passed closer to the physical world? They often do not bring proof that is necessary for people that are either visiting the Spiritualist Church the first time or having a sitting with the Medium. In your opinion are these mediums not having enough training and carrying out sittings before they are ready, who may not be doing justice to the truths and the teachings of the Spirit World?"

Khan: "There are many souls who are going through their first passing, who desire to communicate again with your world for they feel close to your world. These souls have not yet shaken off the chains and garments of the physical world. They still feel the bonds with your world, It is not wrong for these souls, likewise it is not wrong for souls within your world to seek comfort from the souls which have passed through to our side, you must not judge others, if they go for entertainment, then make their entertainment of an illuminating nature, there are many souls trying to carry out the work within your world, there are many of an unenlightened nature, this is their own path, they try to the best of their abilities, but there are many within your world who try to falsify which they know, they try to mislead people, they try to benefit from the souls, unenlightened souls within your world, this is why we stress it is important for you to use this knowledge and this creative force for the benefit of others.

Mediumship is a two-way communication; we cannot work without you and you cannot work without us. New Mediums have much to learn but also their Guides have much to learn as they are trying to find a way of communication that both can work with.

Some ways may not be desirable for everyone and Guides and Mediums will learn to work together, and spirit will find a way that suits both. For a new medium it is not so easy, but it is easier from our side, for we see much clearer. It is harder in the physical world for you are working blind, for spirit can see much more of the eternal plan and the eternal laws, which surround everything, so we find it much easier and we have a greater sense of freedom of mind than you do, for you are working on two levels, whereas we only work on the one level, for we are purely mind.

There are many things which we would like to say to you, but we know that the time is not right, we say one thing in passing, that the other so called established churches or gatherings in your world, serve a purpose for certain souls, do not chastise these churches for there are many within your own church and beliefs who came from these churches as they form a foundation.

Everything has a purpose if you just look. Everything has an opposite, there is a creative force, there is also a destructive force, there is a Heaven and there is a Hell, these reside within each of you, you make your own heaven and you make your own hell. It is up to you which attitude you choose to use.

We hope that you will still radiate the lights from your hearts which you do as you continue to gather knowledge; we will try to surround you in the light of knowledge. We know your difficulties, that is why we feel honoured that you allow us the time to speak to you, to use you, for we know the difficulties within your world, we cry when we see injustices, but within your world, we know that within your hearts there is the means to cure injustice and to spread the word of love, for without love nothing could exist, for without light nothing can grow, the seed is planted in darkness but it stretches towards the light, for in the light it finds everything which it needs. Use your flowers in your gardens as symbols and keep the flowers within your hearts and you will never go wrong. God   Bless."

28: Spirit Visitors within our Circle

Occasionally we had other souls who would come and join our Circle with the help of our Spirit Guides to guide them and to communicate through them to bring some knowledge or to transmit their experiences from the spirit world.

I have transcribed the conversations as they have been dictated on the recording … sometimes there are pauses and gaps but that is normal in conversations. Below are some excerpts of conversations or communications from Spirit visitors:

Soul Visitor A: "Become like masters, ready to do thy will and become pure light to be able to reflect the best that there is within life, that you should not shirk your responsibilities, that you should see within life the good of working for others, that you should see to heal the sick, that you should seek to be aware of all those in troubled states. That you should be aware that the world in which you live is going through many changes. The dark times are coming, but those with this knowledge will know that there is the light that sustains all things within your world as you walk within your pathways of life.

You will then understand, that, there are many things put in your way and your pathway to show you the light of love and to make you strong to prepare you for being channels of the truth. Channels for the Spirit people to work with. Some have experienced the truth and others are on the pathway of experiencing. Then, many people go forward and see that light within your lives that can uplift you and uphold you through all the many difficulties of your lives, in this way, you become a purer channel for the spirit to work with and the days gone by, the light of spirit was much easier, people didn't have your problems, they are now replaced by other problems and yet, the human condition yells out for the light, it does not know where it can go to be sustained by the very light of love and harmony. For, in the darkness people walk in a maze and they do not understand that the spirit people are trying to make their lives better and if you look back in your lives, you will understand that the spirit people have brought you through many trials and it is not our fault for everything that goes wrong for this is the human condition. This is the problem of being human, but you must remember that there are many souls in the spirit home that wish to manifest upon the earth at this time. You are very lucky to be upon the earth at this time although you are going through many difficulties individually.

When you pass from your world, there are many people who will meet you, who will greet you with the love that you cannot imagine yet upon the earth and yet, these people are around you now and want to tell you that they are with you and helping you go forward in your lives. For, many times you discover the difficulties of living, but, remember you have food, you have water, you have many things in your lives that other souls do not possess and you have been put in particular positions of responsibility and because we cannot speak the message through the churches then it will come through the groups and as people sit in their various groups they will feel the love and the harmony and we will take from these groups, but we will give back to each one in their respective time the energy and the love which is taken, for it is taken from here and used to help those who cry out for wisdom, who cry out for food and who cry out for spiritual sustenance.

Many times people turn away from the spirit world and many times they will return and many times they will leave and return but, when it is their time they will stay, but, we only go with those who will stay, those of you that stay for a short time do not get the full benefit of the spirit world and of the spiritual energies. Those who stay on this pathway through trials and tribulations are of the ones that will help others to progress and so we are able to roll away the stone of ignorance and let people see the marvellous colours that you blend and let people be aware that as you sit, you blend in colours, you are each of the colours and the green colour is most important, for that is the balance that is the healing that is the calmness. When you are calm, nothing will disturb you, we bring the love of the spirit people towards you and we send blessings as you sit in your group waiting for something to happen, but, you are the instigators, you are the active, you are the participants, you are part of the whole you are the strength of the spirit. We need you as much as you use us."

Khan "There is another here this evening who is trying to communicate, he asks if it will be allowed for him to learn with you...for we teach on our level, we have said before that we learn from you, it is not often we find the chance to join with your world, it is not often we find souls in sympathy with ourselves. It is hard for me to judge, for I find it hard to communicate with your world, for there are so many thought patterns that I must use to get through to you. I use many terms which I find in the first communicators mind (The Guide Bhatti) which are sometimes alien to me. I use odd terms of a Buddhist nature for I am not of that belief myself, so we find it hard for we can only use what we find within that soul, we cannot impress things upon you which are not there already, the soul, he wishes to communicate."

Soul Visitor B: "Thank you! I do hope that it is not too much trouble for me to be here this evening. I find it very hard. I cannot get a lot ... (he pauses) ...you wish to know where I originate?

I come from the land which surround the Red Sea. I find it very hard to be with you this evening. I need much help. It is only thanks to the souls that are around me this evening, I try to learn many things, we are told that we receive a great deal from the willingness to help you and I find it easier knowing that there is help from both sides of the veil. I feel very happy to be here this evening, I do have a great deal which I can tell you which may help you but, I can try to encourage you all by saying that I thought that at the time of my death, that I would cease to exist, for in your world I was not a very good man, and unfortunately I drank quite a lot and I mistreated people. These are things that I regret, but, I speak to you this evening to say that you do carry on, your life is much enriched when you find yourselves on the other side, there are so many things which I have to learn and there are so many that I wish to do for now. I realise, that I was wrong in the things I did in your world, and this is my chance to try and help the people in your life, by telling you of the things which you may find on the other side. I hope that it is not too much trouble, for I do not know a great deal, there are so many people around me who know a lot more, who could give you a lot more.

I appreciate the opportunities; I thank our chance to have been with you. Please do not forget that you are important to us. We need you. Only this is the only way that we can find redemption. Thank you for listening. "

Khan. "It is not always that we get the chance to bring these Souls. For it is not always that we can find a gathering of your abilities and your sensitivities. We are pleased the way you conduct yourselves, but you must remember that everything which you do in your lives should reflect the way you believe. Try not to make too many mountains within your world, for as you already know, that your lives are of your own making. So, you must live your lives as pure and as enlightened as you can. We pray that each of you will shine forth and will be a beacon for all the things in your life that mean so much to so many, and we know that your work will bring an end to the strife within your world, an end to the misunderstandings within your world, there is only one dharma (to do something without expectation of reward from others). There is only one law. Not many people follow this law, they need guides, they need the wisdom, wisdom comes from the heart that it can lead from fall through love and through the good things which you already have within your hearts. The Guides are saying that these plants (the people within our Circle) are in full bloom, and he enjoys the scent that these flowers give, it is a beautiful thing to look at within the garden. We know that you are the garden, that you are well kept and are being cultivated but the growing you must do yourselves.

29: General Questions and Answers

Questioner: "It has always puzzled me about eating meat. Is it right to eat meat?"

Khan: "Do you yourself feel it is wrong?"

Questioner: "I do yes"

Khan: "Then it is wrong, for it is your own teachings, it is your own path which you must follow. If you found that it was right to eat meat, then it would be right. But it would only be right for you. It is wrong for you to try to enforce this teaching on others, but we must say that we have impressed upon my communicator that it is right not to eat meat of any sort, for it is right for him, we would not give this guidance if we felt it would harm him in any way, but it is only right for him, but I also feel it is wrong, to take the life of anything, but that is my own beliefs, drawn from experiences within your world. Have you asked yourself why you do not eat meat?

You are impressed with the thought that it is wrong to eat meat. "

Questioner: "It is the thought of killing something."

Khan: "You have a Guide of an evolved nature who is close to you, he is of the Hindu teachings, he is of the KRSNA teachings. And this guide will impress his thoughts upon you. He will not try to enforce them, but he is close to you, so you pick up his thoughts, this is how we impress."

Questioner: "I have had him for a very long time now, for quite a few years."

Khan: "There are guides with each of you which give strength and guidance, the teachings and healing. You can call upon these guides at any time."

Questioner: "There is also another question, I would like to know about my Guide, please…"

Khan: "Which Guide do you refer?"

Questioner: "I don't know how many I've got." Khan: "You have many, each of you have many guides. You have many guides who teach many different things. The guide who you will choose to work with you all have their answers for the needs of the moment."

· *Questioner*: "How do I choose?"

Khan: "By the life you live. You need the philosophies and you need the teachings of the spirit world, so you may take a greater step. So, the Guides you refer will be of a philosophical nature, which you have three of varying degrees."

Questioner: "When sometimes I first wake up in the mornings, answers come in clearer to me just as I wake up … They seem like a dream, but they are not…"

Khan: "When you wake up in the mornings, you will find many things, you will see answers, you will get answers to things, the instant you wake. You will all realise within your sleeping periods you dwell within the Astral World, for your mind withdraws from the physical world and abides within the next manifestation of the self, which is and which some call Heave, and some call the Astral World.

This is part of yourself, you are dwelling within the realms of your spirit, so you will know things. You will experience things of a much higher degree. When you wake the memory is still with you until the physical world takes root once more. It is important for you to be of the physical world but not dwell upon the physical world." Chapter 30: More teachings from Khan Friends, your beliefs in the endless light and the continuation of consciousness must be your props in your world. You must use your spiritual knowledge, setting down your roots, and draw upon the food of knowledge to nourish your hearts. The bigger the roots, the stronger the bow. The winds of change are blowing around you. Through firm foundations, spirit in the knowledge of everlasting love, you can bend the wind of change. It will not blow too strong for your roots to withhold. It is written in your book "seek and you shall find", this has many implications.

Each one of you has embarked on a journey, an everlasting journey. At first you fumble about in the dark. The knowledge is the key. With the key brings the light which illumines the path. Each of you searches for the key in different ways. This is good. You must remember this. You must use your lives as a learning period. All experiences teach.

As a tree grows upwards and sends many bows to the light, you must use this as a symbol in your lives. Firm roots, healthy trunk, many bows. Within the plant there is many uses of a physical nature, within the trees there are many uses of a spiritual nature. You must look at all things, you must see all uses and all purposes, you must look at one another and see the uses and the purposes within each person. Each person has a use and a purpose in life, through determining your own purposes. You can become aware of the uses and lives of others.

Everything has a purpose; everything has a life. Search for these things. Use the light to illumine your own lives and your own world so you may see them in a new way. Your problems are not problems. As a guide for your lives we cannot rule your lives, we cannot live your lives for you. Our aim is guidance, and the teachings of experience. There are many Guides around you, which you can call upon. They all give the same messages, but in a different way, for they come from different experiences and different outlooks. They all search for the same thing.

Within the hearts of each of you there is a so-called instinct - within all mankind there are instincts. Each man in your world searches for something. If the search is with an unenlightened heart and mind that is the fumbling in the dark.

Many people search for things. They do not know for which they search. There is a restlessness within them. There are many people who supplement this restlessness with base emotions and base needs. Many times, we speak of the envious kind, many times we speak of the jealous kind. This is their search. They know what they search for. They gather all things and are envious of all things, for their outlook on life is of an unenlightened nature.

Each person treads a different path, it is wrong to criticise another's path. You must look at your own path and use the ground that you have gained, for the advantages of others. For each one of you in this room, - your knowledge and experience come from different backgrounds and different lives and different lessons learned and from lessons to be learned. Each one of you is right in your search for your own path, which leads to the same destination. So do not look at each other's paths and say, "you must tread this way".

Many teachers in your world proclaim this as the work of God. If this was the work of God each person would have the same burdens, each person would have the same beliefs, each person would have the same background. We are impatient with the people who proclaim this, for this is not spirits teachings. When we enter your existence, we feel the same old emotions, but we have the knowledge of the spiritual realms. Sometimes it is not easy. We regret these emotions when entering your world for we passionately strive for the ultimate. We try to show all obstacles when entering your existence. We see the wrongs in your world and feel sad and we feel angry. These are wrong emotions and we apologise. But use this as a teaching and not let your emotions overrule your mind.

We learn from the physical world whereas we hope you learn from ours. There are many people in your life who try to impress wrong teachings and wrong thoughts. There are many in your world of an unenlightened nature who follow these people for there is restless within their hearts, and the shackles and the chains of their physical existence. It makes it hard for their spiritual body to shine through. When the realisation comes about that, you choose your own lives. You can reflect on your lives and you can see the phases in your life that need alteration. This is one more step on the path of life. For the longest journey starts with a single step, this is often the hard step. It says in one of your books, I think the reference is in the Book of James, it says ' 'If any of you lack knowledge, ask and upbraid not, and it shall be given.' This is a promise from a Master. When the seed develops to a sufficient stage within your heart, you will all gain a master who will teach you to the level of his development. Do not look for these masters, but as you read your books and as you live your lives, if something strikes you and it makes you think and reflect, these are the teachings which you should follow. But never forget always use these teachings and if they prove false within your lives, reject these teachings for these are false teachings from false masters. The master Buddha taught of the continuation of the mind, and the continuation of the consciousness. This is the soul; you must look for the soul in all things. This is symbolised in the following as the "Wheel of Life". You must regard all your lives as one continuous wheel without beginning and without end, use this wheel to travel. The spokes of a wheel lead to the hub, within the hub you will find the pool of all things, all knowledge, all teachings. You travel around the rim of the wheel; each spoke indicates a previous life. All lives lead to the whole, to the hub. Use these symbols and use the knowledge of all Masters. Whether they be of one faith or following or whether they be of another faith or cultural background, it makes no difference. All cultures have been given a specific truth, all cultures in this time are drawing close to each other. There is a new dawn, there is a new form of existence within your world at this time. This has brought about a knowledge of all things and souls of a like mind, of a developed nature of minds, devout enough to comprehend the teachings of the spirit world and to throw down the boundaries between race and creed.

Boundaries limit! Any teaching or any life that has its boundaries is a false following or a false teaching. The nations of your world are starting to throw down their boundaries. As each day passes within your lives the threat of war within your world decreases at every moment. This is no accident; this is brought about because of the new age dawning within your lives. Many people within your world have taught of this, but this is only brought about through the understanding of enlightened souls who try and strive for a greater understanding of the self and use this knowledge for enlightenment within your own cultures.

Draw from whatever source you need, if it is of a good nature. Just because a plant comes from one part of the world it does not mean its beauty is any less than a plant found within your own gardens. The bulb of that plant may differ, and the cultural backgrounds within all your humanity may differ, deep within your heart it is the same. We have said before: do not criticise your neighbour's garden until your own garden is in order. Thus, you will only teach up to your knowledge, for you cannot teach of things which you have no understanding. When you have that understanding, all is clear, all is orderly, and nobody can doubt your words. We pray your roots will delve deep within your home or own hearts and that you will use the fruit of knowledge for the nourishment for that part and that bough to be strong enough to withstand the wind of change. You may bow and you may bend, but through the knowledge of the spirit world you will not break. We hope this is useful, we pray that you understand.

30: More teachings from Khan

Friends, your beliefs in the endless light and the continuation of consciousness must be your props in your world. You must use your spiritual knowledge, setting down your roots, and draw upon the food of knowledge to nourish your hearts. The bigger the roots, the stronger the bow. The winds of change are blowing around you. Through firm foundations, spirit in the knowledge of everlasting love, you can bend the wind of change. It will not blow too strong for your roots to withhold. It is written in your book "seek and you shall find", this has many implications.

Each one of you has embarked on a journey, an everlasting journey. At first you fumble about in the dark. The knowledge is the key. With the key brings the light which illumines the path. Each of you searches for the key in different ways. This is good. You must remember this. You must use your lives as a learning period. All experiences teach.

As a tree grows upwards and sends many bows to the light, you must use this as a symbol in your lives. Firm roots, healthy trunk, many bows. Within the plant there is many uses of a physical nature, within the trees there are many uses of a spiritual nature. You must look at all things, you must see all uses and all purposes, you must look at one another and see the uses and the purposes within each person. Each person has a use and a purpose in life, through determining your own purposes. You can become aware of the uses and lives of others.

Everything has a purpose; everything has a life. Search for these things. Use the light to illumine your own lives and your own world so you may see them in a new way. Your problems are not problems. As a guide for your lives we cannot rule your lives, we cannot live your lives for you. Our aim is guidance, and the teachings of experience. There are many Guides around you, which you can call upon. They all give the same messages, but in a different way, for they come from different experiences and different outlooks. They all search for the same thing.

Within the hearts of each of you there is a so-called instinct - within all mankind there are instincts. Each man in your world searches for something. If the search is with an unenlightened heart and mind that is the fumbling in the dark.

Many people search for things. They do not know for which they search. There is a restlessness within them. There are many people who supplement this restlessness with base emotions and base needs. Many times, we speak of the envious kind, many times we speak of the jealous kind. This is their search. They know what they search for. They gather all things and are envious of all things, for their outlook on life is of an unenlightened nature.

Each person treads a different path, it is wrong to criticise another's path. You must look at your own path and use the ground that you have gained, for the advantages of others. For each one of you in this room, - your knowledge and experience come from different backgrounds and different lives and different lessons learned and from lessons to be learned. Each one of you is right in your search for your own path, which leads to the same destination. So do not look at each other's paths and say, "you must tread this way".

Many teachers in your world proclaim this as the work of God. If this was the work of God each person would have the same burdens, each person would have the same beliefs, each person would have the same background. We are impatient with the people who proclaim this, for this is not spirits teachings. When we enter your existence, we feel the same old emotions, but we have the knowledge of the spiritual realms. Sometimes it is not easy. We regret these emotions when entering your world for we passionately strive for the ultimate. We try to show all obstacles when entering your existence. We see the wrongs in your world and feel sad and we feel angry. These are wrong emotions and we apologise. But use this as a teaching and not let your emotions overrule your mind.

We learn from the physical world whereas we hope you learn from ours. There are many people in your life who try to impress wrong teachings and wrong thoughts. There are many in your world of an unenlightened nature who follow these people for there is restless within their hearts, and the shackles and the chains of their physical existence. It makes it hard for their spiritual body to shine through. When the realisation comes about that, you choose your own lives. You can reflect on your lives and you can see the phases in your life that need alteration. This is one more step on the path of life. For the longest journey starts with a single step, this is often the hard step. It says in one of your books, I think the reference is in the Book of James, it says ' 'If any of you lack knowledge, ask and upbraid not, and it shall be given.' This is a promise from a Master. When the seed develops to a sufficient stage within your heart, you will all gain a master who will teach you to the level of his development. Do not look for these masters, but as you read your books and as you live your lives, if something strikes you and it makes you think and reflect, these are the teachings which you should follow. But never forget always use these teachings and if they prove false within your lives, reject these teachings for these are false teachings from false masters. The master

Buddha taught of the continuation of the mind, and the continuation of the consciousness. This is the soul; you must look for the soul in all things. This is symbolised in the following as the "Wheel of Life". You must regard all your lives as one continuous wheel without beginning and without end, use this wheel to travel. The spokes of a wheel lead to the hub, within the hub you will find the pool of all things, all knowledge, all teachings. You travel around the rim of the wheel; each spoke indicates a previous life. All lives lead to the whole, to the hub. Use these symbols and use the knowledge of all Masters. Whether they be of one faith or following or whether they be of another faith or cultural background, it makes no difference. All cultures have been given a specific truth, all cultures in this time are drawing close to each other. There is a new dawn, there is a new form of existence within your world at this time. This has brought about a knowledge of all things and souls of a like mind, of a developed nature of minds, devout enough to comprehend the teachings of the spirit world and to throw down the boundaries between race and creed.

Boundaries limit! Any teaching or any life that has its boundaries is a false following or a false teaching. The nations of your world are starting to throw down their boundaries. As each day passes within your lives the threat of war within your world decreases at every moment. This is no accident; this is brought about because of the new age dawning within your lives. Many people within your world have taught of this, but this is only brought about through the understanding of enlightened souls who try and strive for a greater understanding of the self and use this knowledge for enlightenment within your own cultures.

Draw from whatever source you need, if it is of a good nature. Just because a plant comes from one part of the world it does not mean its beauty is any less than a plant found within your own gardens. The bulb of that plant may differ, and the cultural backgrounds within all your humanity may differ, deep within your heart it is the same. We have said before: do not criticise your neighbour's garden until your own garden is in order. Thus, you will only teach up to your knowledge, for you cannot teach of things which you have no understanding. When you have that understanding, all is clear, all is orderly, and nobody can doubt your words. We pray your roots will delve deep within your home or own hearts and that you will use the fruit of knowledge for the nourishment for that part and that bough to be strong enough to withstand the wind of change. You may bow and you may bend, but through the knowledge of the spirit world you will not break. We hope this is useful, we pray that you understand.

31: Inspirational Quotes

During the sittings within our Circle. When it was time for our Circle Spirit Guide to leave us until the next time, he quoted Inspirational Quotes to inspire and remind us of who we all are and how we should live our lives.

I would like to share these with you and hope that you feel the love and understanding that we all felt.

"God Bless you all, I would like to say, as the love flows through, we wish to talk of tolerance amongst you, and amongst all the people of your earth plane, we ask only that you keep your hearts open to the other vibrations on your earth plane, that you may give out only your love and never judge, and never condemn another fellow man. The true work is love, there are many people in their development at different levels and it is hard for you to understand their plight, but you must be patient with these people, my friends, they need your understanding and your love, there is much hurt and many cruel words spoken. You understand, just remember, never to judge others" … Khan

"Do not forget within your lives, the simple things can be as precious as anything you experience for do not forget that a lump of coal is but a young diamond, is this not true? We pray that you will use the colours which surrounds each of you, there are a village of beautiful flowers around each of you. All you have got to do is to see these without seeing. We pray that your hearts will be filled with the gladness and the love which abounds, we are grateful for the moments we share with you and we are proud to be associated with you. We leave you in the pure light of love. God Bless."

"We thank you for your time. We pray that you will keep on the enlightened path and will not get lost down the alleys and byways in your lives. We pray that you will attune yourselves in accord with the celestial choirs, you are one part of that choir and we need you, and we need you in tune so the whole will be in chord, so you will all sing the same, we do not need discord, and we pray you will find this. God Bless.... Khan

"Each one of you go through trials, do not forget the flowers by the roadside, the flower struggles to gain the roots, but it still blossoms. May you gather all which you need within this life to add to your own individual garden, so you may show the unenlightened souls of your world the beauties which abound all around, you must sing out with joy at the things which you have, not the things with which you wished you had. God Bless. "Within each of you lies the true nature of spirit, within each of you is the pure bounteous light of all creation, within each of you are all the answers of everything which you care to ask. The only thing which stops you from gaining these answers and gaining this light is the physical world. The misconceptions and the false teachings of the physical world. It is all about you, you must look at the nature, you must look at the animal kingdom." God Bless

"We leave you now, we pray that it will continue that we will be able to drink in your happiness, that we may be able to bathe in the love which you show us. For we hope that the diamond, precious of all things, is the most precious thing within your world, it has many facets as there are souls that shine like the diamond, and we are very grateful for this. We are grateful for the warmth that you show us from your lives. God Bless."

"Everything has a purpose if you just look. Everything has an opposite, there is a creative force, there is also a destructive force, there is a Heaven and there is a Hell, these reside within each of you, you make your own heaven and you make your own hell. It is up to you which attitude you choose to use. We hope that you will still radiate the light from your hearts which you do as you continue to gather knowledge; we will try to surround you in the light of knowledge. We know your difficulties, that is why we feel honoured that you allow us the time to speak to you, to use you, for we know the difficulties within your world, we cry when we see injustices, but within your world, we know that within your hearts there is the means to cure injustice and to spread the word of love, for without love nothing could exist, for without light nothing can grow, the seed is planted in darkness but it stretches towards the light, for in the light it finds everything which it needs. Use your flowers in your gardens as symbols and keep the flowers within your hearts and you will never go wrong. God Bless."

"We leave you, once again, the hopes that you will feel the light and the peace, which abounds each of you. We have said many times that you are very precious, each soul here this evening has many treasures within their heart, share these treasures for these are beautiful gifts which you have. God Bless.

"There is a song within each of your hearts. Do not stifle that song, it is a beautiful song, you each have your own song. Sing out it is a beautiful song, let others hear this song so they may join. So, there within your world there will be a chorus of love of light and peace. God Bless."

"There is need for prayer, for on our side of things the prayer is not of a material thing, Thought is a living thing for everything is taught in your life it is of material and physical, we do not have the physical and material on our side, so thought is a predominant thing, when you send your thoughts out, you call sometimes prayers. they carry and they manifest themselves on our side. Prayers are important in your world; it is not just for the self! God bless."

"Live a life for each day, savour each day for the good things within your life and do not admonish other, live through example which we know you will do, we feel honoured to be working with you. We feel privileged that you accept the teachings which we have and that you call on us, it is a nice feeling, is it not, to be wanted. Each within us, deep within our hearts feels the need to be wanted. This need is from a higher spiritual self, you are all in contact with your higher selves, and one day we all find ourselves within our final home, we pray this will not be too long. God bless."

"We pray that you will honest within yourselves, that you will be able to look through the window without staring at your own reflection. You must look at the beauty within the window of your own hearts and not look at the reflection of the outer self. We know you will carry on the work which we impart within you and we know that your paths of enlightenment will continue. We also know this circle, in whatever form it may find itself, will continue with the souls present here tonight. We leave you in the light of spirit that it may illumine your problems and your pathways. God Bless"

"We are pleased your colours are gaining in lustre all the time, your individual shades and hues are deepening, your colours are no more pastel shades, your colours are rich colours and your colours are with you all the time and we are pleased that you are keeping a balance between the lower colours and the higher colours. We know your soul develop, we know the hard work and this is why we are eternally grateful and this is why we try to be with you as much as we can, for we like to bask in your auras, for in your auras we also gain courage and strength and we pray this will continue. God Bless you"

There is no point in keeping these precious jewels locked within the vault, everything of beauty must be shown, you cannot appreciate beauty if you cannot see it, you must let your talents shine so others may see the light and may join you on your own path, for you can give them encouragement so they can proceed down their own path. Each of you are precious, we have said before we are honoured to be working with you, for we find a great sympathy within each of you. We leave you, once again, the hopes that you will feel the light and the peace, which abounds each of you. We have said many times that you are very precious, each soul here this evening has many treasures within their heart, share these treasures for these are beautiful gifts which you have. God Bless.

Let your hearts shine, let the people within your world see the light within you, so they may want to take up the path of light which you have already burnished, we pray that as you look up to the heavens and you see the stars and you see the wonder of your world, you will take this as a reminder of the promises and the gifts which are to come. We leave you draped with love and peace and with a great sense of gratitude.

You can only live one day at a time for there is only one day for you to live at a time. You do not live five or six days every day. You must look around your world and pick your lessons. They are there. There are many lessons you overlook.

You must also think that the lives that you lead are of your own making. You chose the time and the place and the life which you live is of your own making. Life is not what you see through your eyes. Life is what you feel, for the biggest problem within your world is to teach people, they are not what they see. these are two-dimensional people, they do not see their inner self, they cannot think of things to come and things past. This is your hardest work. You must illuminate. We are pleased for we know the effort which goes into this work, we have also been through these lives and we are grateful for the opportunity that you give to us to teach. God Bless

"If these words fit within your life and enrich your life, drink of it as you will, so it may nourish the seed within, so that your own spiritual growth will come into bloom. But take only from these words that which you need and question all. Do not accept anything until you have questioned. This is not the ONLY truth but one of many truths. If you find these words do not fit in with your life, then it is not for you... I hope and pray that you will find your pathway. But remember Question All. Only then, will you find what is right for you. ...khan

32 Glossary of Terms

Bodhisattva: a person who can reach Nirvana (a transcendent state released from the cycle of rebirth) but refuses to do so through compassion for suffering beings.

Dharma: In Buddhism -The nature of reality regarded as a universal truth taught by the Buddha.

Doorkeepers: Doorkeepers are souls who look after each living soul. They protect and care for us. They will not let anything come to us or near us that will harm us. They are not beings of a true advanced nature; but they are loving and caring souls. The Spirit world cannot go against their will. There are laws in the Spirit World which only we in Spirit must obey and there are laws in the Spirit World which only peoples of the earth have to obey. Doorkeepers are not Spirit Guides.

Spirit Guides: Spirit guides are teachers. Spirit Guides are the ones that give us the understanding. Our Guides (and we all have one or more) are still with us when we pass into the Astral World. They are from a higher Spiritual level above the Astral World. We are never alone.

Nishkam Karma: Means to act unselfishly, or without personal gain. Prana: Means the Sanskrit word for breath, 'life force', or 'vital principle'.

NOTES

Printed in Great Britain
by Amazon

75659202R00073